Crash and Learn:
600+ Road-Tested Tips to Keep Audiences
Fired Up and Engaged!

Jim Smith Jr.

Alexandria, VA

12   11   10   09   08   07   06   1   2   3   4   5   6   7

ASTD Press is an internationally renowned source of insightful and practical information on workplace learning and performance topics, including training basics, evaluation and return-on-investment (ROI), instructional systems development (ISD), e-learning, leadership, and career development.

Ordering information: Books published by ASTD Press can be purchased by visiting our website at store.astd.org or by calling 800.628.2783 or 703.683.8100.

Library of Congress Control Number: 2006939561

ISBN-10: 1-56286-465-3
ISBN-13: 978-1-56286-465-1

ASTD Press Editorial Staff
Director: Cat Russo
Manager, Acquisitions & Author Relations: Mark Morrow
Editorial Manager: Jacqueline Edlund-Braun
Senior Associate Editor: Jennifer Mitchell
Associate Editor: Tora Estep
Editorial Assistant: Kelly Norris

Copyeditor: Karen Eddleman
Indexer: April Davis
Proofreader: Kris Patenaude
Interior Design and Production: Kathleen Schaner
Cover Design: Steve Fife

Printed by Victor Graphics, Inc., Baltimore, Maryland, www.victorgraphics.com.

Contents

Foreword

Crash and Learn is an amazing book. I wish I would have had it 20 plus years ago when I started training in corporate America!

I have observed all the trainer mistakes that Jim Smith writes about:

- Seeing themselves as the sole experts and disregarding what the trainees bring to the table
- Doing a data dump and assuming it's effective training
- Setting up the room in classroom style and assuming interaction will naturally occur
- Losing control of the session and then blaming it on a "bad group"
- Allowing technology to drive the training (made even worse when the technology fails)
- Co-facilitators stepping all over each other.

The bad news is that these scenarios continue to happen every day. The good news is that Jim Smith has written this book. It is an easy read and especially well organized. It can be a "bible" for new trainers and a refresher course for seasoned trainers.

I remember when I was still teaching college full time and starting to do corporate training. I spoke to the sociology department about the value of interaction, facilitation, and adult learning in the classroom. The response of the audience members was "You are right, but if we do this, how do we give them the necessary information in the allotted amount of time?" My response, "Is your goal to give it, or that they 'get it'?"

Crash and Learn will help them get it. This book is a valuable resource—it should be required reading for all trainers.

Marjorie Brody, CSP, CMC, PCC
CPAE Speaker Hall of Fame
Founder and CEO, BRODY Professional Development
Jenkintown, PA

Preface

As I sat pensively at the trainer's table in the back of the room, observing my co-facilitator painstakingly deliver her workshop segment, I began to think she needed to do one or more of the following, and quickly:

- take a break to regroup
- do a lot more listening and a lot less talking
- pray for divine intervention
- acknowledge to the participants that the workshop was not going as planned and ask for their assistance in righting the ship.

I signaled to her to give the group an assignment, thinking that a brief huddle-up with me would allow us to discuss the sinking ship that was once our workshop. Instead, she shot me a look that shouted, "I can handle this without your help, Jim" and continued her monotone death by lecture.

Frustrated participants started to turn in their chairs to look at me in the hope that I would rescue them. Discontent dripped from every team table. There were more sighs, groans of exasperation, and side conversations than one would find in a doctor's crowded waiting room. She went on for another 45 minutes before she gave the group a much-needed break. They rushed out of the room, not even waiting to hear how long the break would be. I made a beeline toward her to provide what I thought would be useful feedback. She paid less attention to me than a husband pays to his family while reading the newspaper at the dinner table.

After the workshop, we spoke briefly, but all she wanted to discuss was how rude and unreceptive the participants were during her presentation.

I was astonished! Were we in the same room? What did I miss? Did I need a new prescription for my glasses?

That disastrous workshop occurred more than 10 years ago, but I remember it like it happened yesterday. From that point on, I started writing down the mistakes that trainers, including myself, make in the classroom. The result is the book in your hands.

The Pain of Presenting

Which do you think is most challenging: walking five miles in two feet of snow without any shoes during a blustery Minnesota winter evening; driving in a New York City traffic jam with four flat tires, a faulty air conditioner, and a near-empty gas tank on a sweltering summer afternoon; sitting in coach class between a snorer and a talk-a-holic and in front of a crying baby during an eight-hour flight; or facilitating a workshop with a room full of disinterested, distracted, and annoyed participants? I have never walked in snow without footwear, and I avoid driving in New York City traffic. When I fly, I prefer the aisle and window seats unless, of course, I'm able to upgrade to first class. Nevertheless, just like many of you, I have been in a training room as a participant, facilitator, and observer, with disinterested, distracted, and annoyed participants. I think I would prefer any of the other three scenarios to death by lecture. Moreover, the bad taste lasts longer when we, as trainers and facilitators, are the guilty parties who created the lethargic, disempowering climate.

I'd rather have root canal without Novocain than hear trainers play "Blame the Victim." You've heard it before: "That was a tough group." "They were brutal." "I couldn't do anything to loosen them up." "I'm glad I don't have to be in front of them again." The truth—the whole truth and nothing but the truth—is that we are, more times than not, responsible for making participants want to shout, sleep, or sneak out of the classroom.

I have been in the training and development field for more than 20 years. I have worked for major organizations in the corporate arena and for several notable training and consulting companies. I have traveled internationally to lead workshops and have worked with and coached trainers in more than 35 states. I've been to a number of industry conferences as a presenter, speaker, and participant and have observed thousands of trainers, keynoter speakers, and meeting facilitators.

I have observed many awesome trainers and facilitators, but also I have witnessed myriad mistakes. Worst of all, I've even looked up from my own notes from the front trainer's table to see the participants yawning, fidgeting, checking their watches, furtively sending emails on their Blackberry devices, and even sneaking out the back door.

Time to Take Action!

Why do trainers and facilitators continue to persecute audiences? I'd rather believe that most are unaware of their errors—unconscious incompetence—than think that the majority know they're making mistakes and continue to make them anyway. Some of the mistakes are due, in large part, to fear and insecurity despite the apparent abundance of ego in the training business. After all, the privilege of the platform does some crazy things to some people. Certainly, corporate cultures and pressures play a role, too. It's the old, "We've always done it this way" philosophy that makes it so hard to try doing things in new, more engaging ways.

For those reasons and more, I decided to write *Crash and Learn: 600+ Road-Tested Tips to Keep Audiences Fired Up and Engaged!* This book is for trainers, facilitators, teachers, speakers, managers, politicians, lawyers—anyone who has to present information or lead meetings and workshops. *Crash and Learn's* purpose is simple: to help you

- ◆ build connections with your learners and audiences
- ◆ engage your learner's head and heart
- ◆ come across in a polished and powerful way
- ◆ improve your audiences' performance and results
- ◆ create an empowering and motivational learning environment
- ◆ take your training and facilitation skills to heights you've never imagined.

I've written this book to be very reader friendly—almost a quick reference guide. You can start at the beginning, the middle, or the end. Where you begin doesn't really matter; just consider the areas where you think you need the most development and start there.

In each chapter, I first list the specific training/facilitation area, then provide an introductory message, followed by common mistakes and "Jim's Gems"—the ways to correct the mistakes and fire up and engage your audience. Toward the end of each chapter is a piece called "In the Trenches," an up-close anecdote about a trainer in the midst of a mistake. For an additional spark, each chapter concludes with an exercise component that highlights ways to enhance your personal training power and sustain the momentum you gain from this book. Taken together, the exercises make up an application action plan to motivate you to incorporate your new ideas into your training repertoire immediately. The appendix at the end of the book provides an easy-to-complete matrix that will help you bring everything together so you can make the leap to training greatness.

Enjoy your reading. Marinate in Jim's Gems. Make sure you have a highlighter close by.

Repeat after me: No more tension-convention workshops. No more spiritless sessions. No more death by lecture. I'm ready to bury the past! I'm ready to get busy!

Acknowledgments

Many people contributed to *Crash and Learn*. I want to thank my family, Gina, Daecia, Lauren, Jordan, and Ian, who put up with my numerous road trips and my mood shifts but continue to provide never-ending support, understanding, and love. Thanks also to Mom (Nanci Smith): I always say, "I am, because of you. You put the Jim in JIMPACT!" I also wish to thank my giving brother Rodney, who always "has" my back.

I extend my gratitude to all the JIMPACT team members, who continue to provide inspiration, insight, support, laughter, and love: Anthony and Carmen Spann, Kim Forde, Myra Parker, Sharon Rose, Allison Manswell, Dolores Davis, Michael Thompson, Carol Brownlee, Emil Sadloch, Marilyn Massaro, and Yvonne Reid.

Huge shout-outs and thank-yous go out to my Titans. They are incredible people who are always there when I need them. They help keep me healthy—emotionally, spiritually, personally, and professionally: Darren and Cheryl Toliver, Wilma Williams, Raimond and Bionda Honig, Roberta Ross, Connie McCrae Bryant, Bruce Scagel, Toni Hendrix, Arvon Jordan, Barry A. Callender, Maria Garaitonandia, Danny Baeder, Joe Boswell, Aileen Dizon, Amy Sabsowitch, Ceaser and Evelyn Smith, Fayrutz Kirtzman, Jackie Altman, Stephanie Ferguson, Jennifer Weston, Melanie Sallie Dosunmu, Susan Parsons, Kiley Hoffman, Lauren

Slaughter, Lauriann Reynolds, Loraine Ballard Morrill, Lynn Roman, Maria Zywickle, Bob and Missy Hayes, Mike Knoll, Mike Robinson, Nancy Appleman Vassal, Barbara Stern, Patti DeRosa, Mary Mueller, Shantel Ware, Paul Kallmeyer, Brian Prince, Keith Baudin, Sandi Dufault, Kathy Dempsey, Judy Chapman, Griff and Meena Barger, Quincy Bosman, Renee Russell, Shelly Michas, Steve and Judy Kane, Theresa Krallinger, Uve Coles, Yolanda Rocio Fleming, Diane Chew, and Jeanne Bray, Kathy Thomas, Kristin Black, and Julie Johnson.

I'd also like to thank my clients, customers, and partners (notably AstraZeneca, MetLife, Subaru, Johnson and Johnson, PCR, Commerce Bank, ED FUND, Simmons Associates, Fired Up, and ASTD) for having the confidence in me to JIMPACT their employees and for providing opportunities for me to grow as a speaker, trainer, and person. Thank you, Deb Ventura and Katherine Repetti. Thank you, Brad Bodell, Nancy Stella, and Rose Johnston. Thank you, Tom Steely, Beth Perez, Linn Calder, and Denise Brennan. Thank you, Mary Ann D'Angelo, Mike Burczak, Leigh Ann Hayes, and Bill Driscoll. Thank you, Cindy Pautzke and Shannon Percy. Thank you, Crystal Reilly, Shannon Peck, and Tim Bouch. Thank you, John Dodson. Thank you, Terry and Tony Simmons. Thank you, Gena Carter and Rodney Morris. Thank you, Linda David. Thank you for your feedback.

Dedication

This book is dedicated to my best friend, soul mate, sweetheart, and angel, Gina M. Williams. Gina, ever since we met in ninth grade, in 1975, you have always been there for me. I will always cherish our special love. Thank you for loving me, supporting me, and believing in me. You make my heart smile.

Jim Smith Jr.
December 2006

1

Facilitation Mistakes

Great facilitators are a wonder to watch. They keep a meeting or training event lively and productive even as they effortlessly fend off efforts from participants to take over the meeting, derail the positive mood, or otherwise disrupt a successful event. You may have thought to yourself, "How do they do this? I am actually enjoying this meeting!"

Although this chapter does not promise to teach you how you can develop into a world-class professional facilitator, it does reveal 21 of the most common mistakes that most experienced facilitators and trainers would agree could sink any meeting or event no matter how well it is going.

These mistakes span the facilitation blooper landscape from using inappropriate humor to ignoring obvious tension in the room to ending late. Successful facilitation is a delicate balance of keeping a strong hand on the proceedings while understanding and using human psychology to your advantage. Some mistakes you will recognize immediately as something you have experienced, whereas others may confirm what you already know through experience. Others may come as surprise because you've seen so many trainers and speakers incorporate them in their delivery. As you read the mistakes along with Jim's Gems, determine which miscues you must eliminate from your training repertoire to create more spirited, successful, and productive sessions. The exercise at the end of the chapter will help you begin that process.

Mistake #1:
Not opening the session in a strong, memorable way

Jim's Gems:

- Whenever possible, avoid waiting for people. If you must wait a few minutes (never more than 10), give your learners a brief content-related activity.

- Because a solid opener is extremely important to getting your session off on a positive and inspirational note, consider telling a story, sharing a powerful quote, or facilitating a get-up-out-of-your-seat activity, or sharing a surprising, related, powerful statistic.

- Put on a skit with your co-facilitator highlighting your expectations for the session. Have some fun with it. Poke fun at some of the ups and downs you've experienced when conducting this session in the past. The key is to pretend that your audience members are not in the room.

- Pique the learners' curiosity with table props and an empowering room setup.

- Create connections and conversations by putting your participants in activities where they have to share learning goals, expectations, questions, and get-to-know-you information.

- Pay a candid compliment, share your enthusiasm and experience, or ask a challenging question.

- Facilitate an activity in which the learners take personal responsibility and accept accountability and ownership for the learning objectives. Highlight the objectives they have the most interest in and develop questions pertaining to the objectives to encourage them to share the actions they will take to get the most from the day and support each other's learning. Consider pairing participants with learning partners to share their goals and expectations.

> *Lead an assessment activity that allows you to assess the participants' readiness, their knowledge base, their experience, their buy-in, and so forth.*

Mistake #2:
Using inappropriate humor

Jim's Gems:

- ◆ Simply put, don't tell jokes or use inappropriate humor; somebody in your audience will be offended.
- ◆ When attempting to be funny, poke fun at yourself with self-deprecating humor.
- ◆ Simply smile more often; don't take yourself too seriously.

At all costs, avoid using humor related to race, ethnicity, gender, sexual orientation, physical ability, and other diversity-related dimensions; someone in your audience will be offended.

Mistake #3:
Repeatedly calling on the same people during the session

Jim's Gems:

- ◆ Constantly scan the room to make sure you are looking for people who have not participated. Repeatedly calling on the same person will cause others in the room to check out or sit back and move into passive participation. It can also have a negative effect on their self-esteem.
- ◆ Direct certain questions to table groups or people who have not participated much. When you do call on them, make sure your first question is not extremely challenging or they may be reluctant to participate again.
- ◆ Rotate group leaders to get more people involved as leaders.
- ◆ At the workshop's outset, remind the participants that for them to achieve the workshop results they desire, everyone (trainer and participants) has to put some skin in the game. Suggest that they are very much responsible for their personal takeaways and outcomes.

- During breaks, speak to people who have not participated; make sure that they are with you and that nothing else is weighing on their minds.
- Even if someone is contributing great answers or if you have a quiet group, don't play favorites. Repeatedly calling on the same person will lessen the likelihood of someone else volunteering his or her thoughts. The others in the room will just sit back and watch you and your favorite deliver the workshop.

Mistake #4:
Not asking participants to repeat their questions when they ask them

Jim's Gems:

- When a participant asks a question, ask him or her to repeat it so that everyone in the room can hear it. This technique also can buy you some time if you don't have an immediate answer.
- If possible, record participants' questions on a flipchart. Just make sure to get back to them.
- When establishing ground rules, inform the participants that you'd like them to signal you if you fail to repeat a question so that everyone can hear it. The signal could come in the form of someone saying, "I'm sorry, I did not hear the question." Another signal could be someone raising his or her hand.
- Ask other participants to repeat the question or to paraphrase it. This also offers an opportunity for your learners to answer each other's questions.

Mistake #5:
Not providing real-life examples or anecdotes

Jim's Gems:

- Come to every presentation or workshop with real-life current examples and anecdotes to drive home your learning points. Your examples will also give your session more color, energy, and an application focus.
- Ask colleagues, friends, and family members to share their experiences with you.

◆

Record your everyday experiences. You can write them in a book
geared specifically for anecdotes, illustrations, and metaphors.
If you carry a voice recorder, you can record them immediately.
You can also call your voicemail and leave a message
highlighting what you just experienced.

- ◆ Keep a personal journal and review it frequently.
- ◆ Observe others performing the job that you're going to speak about. For example, to acquire some examples, you could go on a sales call with a sales rep or monitor a customer service rep's calls.
- ◆ Attempt to provide at least one anecdote or example every hour. Vary the length. Participants love to hear sincere, real-life examples.
- ◆ To obtain more real-life examples and to see how others cleverly share anecdotes and illustrations with audience members, observe other trainers, speakers, comedians, and others who present on television shows, sports shows, infomercials, and the like.

Mistake #6:
Promising to close the presentation or workshop, then not closing

Jim's Gems:

- ◆ When you tell the group you're going to close or wrap-up, do so. If you don't, you will cause the participants to become restless and they will mentally check out.
- ◆ As you're closing, don't apologize for forgetting some material. In most cases, your audience members will never know you forgot some material.
- ◆ When you're closing, avoid saying, "Oh, one more thing I meant to mention..." Such a statement could prolong your wrap-up, and the participants are very unlikely to retain something you throw in at the last moment when they've probably mentally disengaged anyway.
- ◆ Depending on the length of your session or presentation, you should ask for final questions at least 15-30 minutes before its end. Leave yourself enough time to share your final call to

action. Besides, ending the session by answering or being unable to answer questions is not a powerful way to close.

◆ Don't belabor the close. If you feel the energy in the room has disappeared for good, end the session early. You should always leave your audience members wanting more rather than leaving them feeling as though they had too much.

Mistake # 7:
Going off on a tangent when responding to a question

Jim's Gems:

◆ When you are asked a question, stay on point! Don't attempt to answer multiple questions at once. Your learners will mentally abandon ship if they sense you are getting up on a soapbox. You generally shouldn't take more than a minute or two to answer a question thoroughly.

◆ Look for the participants' reactions to your comprehensiveness. Their body language is often a clear indicator if you have beaten the topic to death.

◆ As you cover the ground rules, establish a "gone off on a tangent" signal that either the facilitator or participants can use. When someone goes off on a tangent, people can hold up a prop (for example, a hammer or clock) to suggest that it's time to move on.

Provide discovery moments for your learners. Refrain from telling them everything. Hold some information back for later in the session. Ask more open-ended, application-based, probing questions. Keep in mind that the session is for the participants. It's not a forum for you to show how much you know.

◆ Ask other participants to attempt to answer the question before you do.

◆ You can provide one answer and then look for others to elaborate on your thoughts.

Mistake #8:
Distributing reading materials or other handouts well before you're going to use them

Jim's Gems:

♦ Only give participants reading materials when you want them to read or review it. Avoid situations where they are reading the material well before you want them to. Once they receive the material, immediately begin to review it or introduce an exercise that allows them to skim it quickly.

When you do distribute handouts or participant guides, introduce them with power and purpose. Give your materials special significance.

♦ When it's time to distribute the handouts, ask for volunteers to come up to your trainer's table to get materials to distribute to the rest of the group.

Mistake #9:
Not providing smooth transitions or clear segues between learning modules

Jim's Gems:

♦ To avoid losing or confusing your participants during transitions between learning modules, you can tell a story, conduct a question-and-answer session, move the group into an activity, ask for volunteers to share their thoughts or observations, or tie the information you just covered into one of the course's learning objectives.

♦ When you're going to move to the next topic, review then preview; that is, tell them what you just told them and tell them what you're going to tell them next.

♦ To make a transition, ask the participants if they know how the material you just covered builds on the information you're about to review.

♦ To segue to the next topic, ask the participants how they're going to apply their new learning back on the job.

Mistake #10:
Facilitating or presenting during distractions

Jim's Gems:

◆ When a distraction occurs, give your learners an assignment to work on at the team tables. You can then go and address the distraction.

◆ If you think the distraction is going to be brief, ask the group to stand to take a quick stretch break. While they're standing, thank them for the work they've done up to that point and encourage them to maintain their focus. You can also stimulate conversation that does not directly pertain to the content.

When a distraction occurs, pause, stop facilitating, and wait for the distraction to end. Distractions always prevent learners from paying attention to the material. Plus, if you pause, you will not have to repeat what you've already presented.

◆ Depending on the type of distraction that's occurring, let the participants know that you're going to wait until the distraction or disruption goes away before you begin facilitating.

◆ Move away from the distraction, perhaps to the opposite side of the room, to take the participants' eyes and attention with you.

◆ During the distraction remain calm; don't raise your voice or try to talk over it.

Mistake #11:
Refusing to defuse the tension in the room

Jim's Gems:

◆ Call attention to the tension. Inform your participants that, as an experienced facilitator, you would be doing them and the organization a disservice if you did not mention that there was tension in the room and say that you won't move forward until the tension is addressed; next ask for their input for how they would like you to address it. When there is tension in the room, learners focus on the tension rather than on the material.

♦

Depending on the kind of tension or distraction, put participants in small groups and have them think of ways to defuse it; record and then discuss their answers.

- ♦ Make sure to thank them for their participation in helping to relieve the tension.
- ♦ If they have concerns regarding the content, assure them that the workshop objectives will address their concerns. Also, tell them that they can speak to you during the break or after the session if they still have concerns.
- ♦ Remind them that, depending on the situation, some tension can be good because it can move people out of their comfort zones.
- ♦ Share a story about a time when early tension in the workshop helped lead to great problem solving, breakthrough thinking, or a sensational session with improved results.

Mistake #12:
Facilitating only from the front of the room

Jim's Gems:
- ♦ Purposefully move around the room periodically as you facilitate but without overdoing it. At some point, every participant should feel as though he or she is sitting at the front of the room. This helps you to better connect with and engage your learners.
- ♦ To switch things up, try initiating the session from the back of the room. You can also try this location after breaks to regain the learners' attention.
- ♦ Facilitate different modules from different parts of the room.
- ♦ Sit on a barstool during debriefing moments; do this from different parts of the room too.
- ♦ Have participants get up and move with you to different parts of the room for your facilitation (this is called changing the venue within the venue).

Mistake #13:
Failing to get the group's attention or get them to quiet down or regroup after a high-energy activity

Jim's Gems:

◆ To get learners' attention immediately use a chime or an instrument that has a distinct sound.

◆ Inform the group that the last one to take his or her seat after the activity will be the first volunteer to review what he or she learned during the activity.

◆ Avoid shouting at the top of your lungs, "Please take your seats!"

◆ Provide a reward for the table group that returns to their seats first and comes to attention.

◆ Use a timer projected onto a screen that serves as an activity countdown.

Before the activity begins, let the group know the signal for reassembling and coming to attention. You could blow a whistle, sound a chime, rise to your feet from your seat, clap your hands, turn the music up or down, or snap your fingers, for example. Having a plan helps you appear like a leader and a polished professional rather than a stressed parent attempting to calm down out-of-control children.

Mistake #14:
Not tapping into the learners' five senses or the variety of learning styles in the room

Jim's Gems:

◆ During your session, alternate between lecture and activity to promote total audience engagement and increased retention.

◆ To tap into the participants' sense of smell, use scented markers as you write on flipcharts or have them use the markers at their tables.

◆ To tap into their sense of hearing, use music.

◆ To tap into their sense of touch and to engage the kinesthetic learners, have them take notes during the session or provide training props and objects (Koosh balls or stress balls, for example) for them to handle.

◆ Provide group problem-solving activities.

◆ Provide brainteasers and activities that require focused thinking.

◆ To tap into the participants' sense of sight, use multiple visual media, such as flipcharts, PowerPoint slides, videos, wall charts, floor charts, handouts, Post-it notes.

◆ Use activities designed for individuals, pairs, small groups, and large groups.

◆ Make sure to allow quiet reflection time, especially during action planning.

◆ To tap into the learners' sense of taste, put candy, chocolate, nuts, fruit, pretzels, or other treats on their tables.

Mistake #15:
Not returning to the learning objectives at the session's conclusion

Jim's Gems:

◆ Plan and facilitate an activity that takes your learners back to the learning objectives as you're wrapping up. Do this without saying, "Let's review the learning objectives." Why? Most participants would rather eat dinner outside during a thunder-storm than hear that they're going to review something they've already discussed—especially at the end of the day. Moreover, your objectives lose their significance if you do not repeatedly refer to them.

◆ During the opening objective's review, have participants think of questions they want answered relative to the course objectives. Have them write the questions in their workbooks or on the back of their name tents. As you're wrapping up the session, spend time reviewing their questions and answers.

A nice touch at the end of your session is to have past participants come in and discuss how they've incorporated the workshop's learning objectives into their jobs.

♦ Near the close of the session, have participants work in small groups to revisit the learning objectives. Instruct them to develop an action or application "next step" for each one.

♦ Close the session the way you began the session and provide a strong call to action. Refer to the learning objectives in your call to action.

Mistake #16:
Not closing the session in a strong, memorable way

Jim's Gems:

♦ Because a strong closer pulls everything together and sends participants off confidently looking forward to applying their workshop learning, consider facilitating a high-energy review activity but without saying, "Let's review...." For example, you could suggest a gallery walk during which the participants create and post their action plans, top challenges, or best practices flipcharts and then walk around surveying or analyzing others' work. Other possibilities include partner sharing, a game of Koosh ball toss, or a team challenge contest using workshop content as the test categories.

Ask them how they're going to adapt, adopt, or apply what they've learned back on the job.

♦ Tell a story.

♦ Have the participants list on a flipchart or in their workbooks what they are going to stop, start, and stay with (or continue doing) because of what they learned.

♦ Provide time for reflection.

♦ Close the session the same way you opened the session.

♦ Facilitate an activity that encourages participants to share their best ideas.

♦ Provide encouraging words that get them looking forward to incorporating their new skills and sharing their thoughts with management.

♦ Avoid closing with questions and answers. The wrong question can sour the atmosphere, leaving a bitter closing taste. Moreover, you might run out of time without thoroughly answering the question.

♦ Share an article relative to industry trends.

♦ Challenge them to take what you've given them to improve both organizational and individual results.

♦ Ask them to complete a self-addressed envelope and to enclose a short list of ideas and to-do items they would like to be reminded about in about a month. You then would mail the envelopes in 30 days.

Mistake #17:
Too much telling, not enough asking (using all lecture and PowerPoint slides) during the session

Jim's Gems:

♦ Because too much telling creates passive learning and relies excessively on one-way communication, at the very least incorporate as many question-and-answer segments as you can. Look for ways to reframe or rephrase the questions you ask.

♦ Use sneaky mini-review activities that the participants won't readily recognize as ways of reviewing the content.

♦ During your session, watch videos and have them experience simulations.

♦ Employ teach-back segments so that you can determine how much the learners have retained.

♦ Have the participants test each other to determine how much they've learned and to see if they can use their reference materials to find the answers.

♦ Provide true/false group quizzes.

♦ Have the participants develop and make group presentations.

Use role plays and case studies to provide feedback; have select participants take on the judging personas of the "American Idol" judges: positive, lukewarm, and constructive-critical.

◆ Provide reading assignments to help individuals process the information they've learned.

◆ To change the workshop's pace, provide quick, fun, spirited activities with wholesome competition.

Mistake #18:
Failing to teach in chunks

Jim's Gems:

◆ To increase learner retention, break your material up into 20-minute chunks. During a 20-minute chunk, use the 3M approach: Material (provide the information or materials), Marinate (give them time to process the information and make it their own), and Memory (check to determine if they are retaining the information). Approximately every 20 minutes, transition the content or your approach to the content. For example, you could facilitate a sneaky review activity, give partic-ipants time to solve a problem, give participants time to share their views or perspectives on the content, give participants reflection time, change your or their positioning, or lead a mini-review discussion.

◆ To maintain the participants' attention, give them a brain-body break every 90 minutes.

◆ Employ the 3M approach when showing a video or leading a PowerPoint presentation too.

◆ Avoid rushing through information or trying to cover too much at one time. Provide links from one module to the next.

Mistake #19:
Failing to send them and get them back from breaks in an inspiring, motivational way

Jim's Gems:

◆ Preview the information you're going to cover upon their return prior to sending them off.

◆ Assign volunteers to make sure their group gets back on time.

- Promise to offer special information that doesn't appear in their workbooks for those who get back early.
- Have an engaging, powerful session up to the break time.
- Have them move around during your session; don't let the break be the first time they're up and around.
- Provide rewards for the first teams to return after breaks.
- If you have created an ongoing competition between teams, take points away from latecomers.

Have latecomers lead review segments by sharing their key learning.

- When possible, conduct one-on-one meetings after you've taken several minutes to regroup.
- Offer more but shorter breaks.
- Give the breaks titles, for example an "email break," a "break to take care of three items on a to-do list," or "a break to check in with one person."
- Provide brainteasers and other trivia activities during the break to encourage people to return quickly.
- Provide questions that will be on the test for the people who get back first.
- Thank them for what they have contributed up to that point.
- Highlight how much they've covered up to that point.
- Facilitate a fun, ongoing, building game. For instance, you can distribute poker cards to the people who get back early. After every break, they receive cards to strengthen their hand. At the end of the workshop, you give a gift to the person who has the best hand.
- Lead special segments during the break during which participants may ask you anything about the content.

Mistake #20:
Ending late

Jim's Gems:
- Reward learners who arrived on time by starting and ending the workshop promptly.

◆

To avoid ending late, make sure to get the session off to a quick start and stay true to the break times given. Don't allow participants to compromise the break time.

◆ To avoid ending late, inform the participants you will be available for 15 minutes after the session to answer additional questions.

◆ Post a parking-lot flipchart or ask-it basket flipchart for participants to post their questions. Quickly follow up within the week with answers to the questions that were not addressed during the session.

◆ Set a personal end-of-content-dissemination time, usually a half hour before the workshop is supposed to end for a full-day session. Use the final half hour to first facilitate 10 to 15 minutes' worth of questions followed by 10 to 15 minutes' worth of closing activities.

◆ Avoid preparing too much content for the time allotted.

◆ Do not overstate your points. Pay attention to your learners' nonverbal messages and energy level. The information you fail to cover can be emailed or sent to them. You can also personally follow up by phone.

Mistake #21:
Failing to see the entire group as your customer

Jim's Gems:

◆ Because it is imperative that your learners believe that you are adding value, facilitate, train, teach, or present to express, not impress.

◆ Take on the role of coach, guide, facilitator, not expert. You should provide information and customer service.

◆ Work to create an environment where your participants leave the session with confidence, energy, and conviction.

- Create plenty of content discovery moments.
- Ask probing, results-oriented, and discovery consulting questions.
- Shift your mindset; train to change behavior and improve results, not to get good evaluations.
- Be authentic, intentional, and consistent.
- Connect with the group.
- Create follow-up opportunities.
- View the entire experience as more than just a training event. Look for methods to help your learners transfer their learning back on the job after the session.

View your participants as the most important people in the room. Put your ego in check.

- Gather as much information as you can about your group before the session. Know their business.
- Provide plenty of feedback and reassuring words.

In the Trenches

I had observed Roz facilitate a number of times. Each time, I walked away shaking my head. We worked for the same consulting firm and sometimes facilitated sessions together and other times observed each other presenting new material. I often thought while watching her facilitate, "How could someone in such an important position of leadership be so clueless about her audience?" Her three favorite words were "me," "myself," and "I." She was a one-dimensional trainer. Everything always had to go her way. If someone tried to provide coaching or feedback, it fell on deaf ears or was met with patronizing replies.

Roz typically began sessions by stating what *her* ground rules were. She wasn't interested in the participants' ground rules. She would then move into her lengthy credibility soliloquy, consisting of 10 pompous minutes on why she was the best trainer to ever sniff a Mr. Sketch marker. Next, she would authoritatively tell her audience members what they were going to learn without ever asking for their input. She would then rifle through the content, occasionally pausing to send participants off to a late break or to answer a question or two. I'd cringe watching her, wondering how long I could stay in the room with her if I weren't getting paid.

On this particular occasion, Roz decided to kick it up a notch. It was a rainy Friday, and management was going to be in the room. Roz was also the project leader for this new client. She was bent on showing them how articulate and polished she was. Beginning in typical Roz fashion, she blew through the ground rules, participant introductions (except, of course, her own), workshop objectives, and the agenda. I was sitting in the back of the room wondering if she knew how she was coming across. I could sense the participants' frustration starting to mount already. "Where did they get her?" I heard one participant ask. "We have to deal with this all day?" "Does she think we're little kids?"

Whether she did or didn't, Roz was in Frank Sinatra's "My Way" form. She talked and talked and talked and talked. They were 15 minutes late in getting to the first break, and then she shortened their break time. During the break, she made small talk with the management team, specifically commenting on how well she thought the session was going.

After the break, the assault continued. Ten-minute modules turned into 40-minute modules. Forty-minute modules turned into 60-minute modules. The class broke late to get to lunch, and Roz suggested that they have a working lunch. Management declined, but lunch was shortened by 15 minutes. The afternoon started much like the morning began. It was the "Roz Show" starring Roz. She purported to know everything about everything. She topped every participant's answer. She always had to get the last word in. She finished their sentences. Her stories and anecdotes droned on interminably.

With less than a half hour remaining in the session, she moved into another activity. I knew at that point that the workshop was going to end late. Sure enough, we finished at 5:30 p.m. instead of 5:00 p.m. People were frustrated. I was annoyed. The rain even seemed to be coming down harder. Roz, however, was unphased, believing she did a commendable job. Afterward, a few management members mentioned to Roz that they were disappointed to be getting out so late. Feeling as though she did the appropriate thing, Roz commented that she wanted them to see the entire program so she didn't think letting out a little late would be a problem.

After that particular session—surprise!—the client requested other facilitators from our team to lead the training.

Building Your Action Plan: Facilitation Mistakes

My top three mistakes are:

1. _____

2. _____

3. _____

My action steps to correct these mistakes are:

1. _____

2. _____

3. _____

I'm committed to correcting these mistakes because:

_____

_____

_____

2

Room Setup Mistakes

When I conduct train-the-trainer sessions, I often remind the participants to make their training room their residence. Whether it's a training room they frequently use or one they're using at another location, it should be spirited, inspirational, and colorful. The same lengths we go to make sure our own homes, spaces, and rooms are well kept and meaningful should be taken when we are preparing our training room for a workshop. Your walls, floors, and chairs have to talk; that is, they should bear purposeful signs. There should be warmth and energy in the space. Participants should walk in and immediately become engaged, intrigued, and excited about what is going to happen.

Unfortunately, many of the training rooms I visit while observing other trainers are plain, spiritless rooms with four walls and a ceiling. The rooms have as much energy as a cell phone with a dead battery. I'm surprised at the number of trainers who undervalue the significance of creating a powerful learning environment—or who just do not create the time to give their training rooms a total makeover. Participants should feel your presence and your difference when they walk into your room. And, they should experience this feeling even if you're not there.

In this chapter, you'll consider some of the most common room setup mistakes that trainers make. From no music to using setups that aren't conducive to interaction and movement, you'll read about what today's trainers and presenters need to stop and start doing to provide the ideal room setup.

Mistake #1:
Failing to have a brief, content-related activity waiting for the participants upon their first entrance into the training classroom

Jim's Gems:

◆ Because learners can be nervous, hesitant, or frustrated about having to attend training, be prepared and have a low-risk, quick icebreaker activity waiting for your participants when they arrive. For example, you could have them list their top three learning goals on the back of their name tent and share them with five people, have them write on the back of their name tent one question that they want answered before the session is over, or have them work in teams to list the wishes and worries they have about the workshop.

Don't be put off by them saying, "You're putting us to work already?" Just smile and say, "Welcome to my place! I'd like your help in getting it ready for the other guests."

◆ To give them a sense of ownership, ask participants to help with a task such as hanging up flipcharts, meeting and greeting others as they enter, writing and posting their favorite quotes, discussing with others their most pressing content-related question and expectations for the workshop upon their entering the room.

◆ Instruct the participants to do some light reading. Place a handout that highlights the workshop's goals and takeaways on their tables or whet their content palate by providing a true/false quiz or a content objectives brainteaser for them to answer.

◆ Have them work in teams to create a list of session ground rules.

◆ Have them think of and share at their tables something old (content they already know about the subject), something new (what they hope to learn during the workshop), something borrowed (something they learned about the subject matter from someone else), and something "blew" (a mistake that they made and have since learned from regarding the subject matter).

Mistake #2:
Using flipcharts in consistent, predictable (boring) ways

Jim's Gems:

- ◆ To attract the learners' attention, hang flipchart sheets on an angle when you post them on the walls.
- ◆ Put content-related or instructional flipcharts on the floor.
- ◆ Use a flipchart with a motivational greeting written on it, as the room's welcome mat. Participants will smile and feel a jolt of inspiration as they walk into the session.
- ◆ Use flipcharts to post questions (ask-it basket, things that make you go hmmmmm, or parking lot issues), best ideas (power points), and wall-worthy words (their sensational sayings) from the session.
- ◆ Post flipcharts with incomplete sentences and have the participants fill in the blanks during the workshop.
- ◆ Avoid starting your session with mundane logistical details for the workshop. Instead, list the session's housekeeping instructions and logistics (bathroom locations, break and lunch times, technical devices dos and don'ts, workshop start and ending times) on a flipchart and hang it under the clock or another place where people frequently look. This way, you don't have to waste precious group time at the beginning reviewing material people can see for themselves.

To capture the eyes of the learners who look up as they mentally check out from time to time, hang content-related or motivational flipcharts on the ceiling; hang them from the ceiling as banners too. Here you can highlight contributions of past participants.

- To deal with zealous early arrivers, post friendly flipcharts on the front door to let them know when you're going to open the door to start the session.
- Post an easel and flipchart near the front door for participants to sign their name if they're ready to contribute to an awesome, memorable session. Your sign should read, "Sign in if you're ready for an awesome workshop."

Mistake #3:
Not arranging tables and chairs appropriately for your training or presentation

Jim's Gems:

- If you want to create more opportunities for interaction, use round tables with four to six people at a table. You can also make this table arrangement with square or rectangle tables by placing the chairs so that no one's back is to the facilitator.

To avoid distractions caused by people entering the room, set up your room so that participants and others enter from the back.

- For presentations, use theater style, U-shape, crescent, or classroom seating.
- If you can, avoid training or presenting in rooms with columns or pillars; they hinder viewing.
- Arrange the tables and chairs so that everyone can have the best possible view of the front of the room and projection screen.

- Arrange the participants' chairs so that their chair backs do not crash into each other when participants get up.

Mistake #4:
No music

Jim's Gems:

- To generate the appropriate energy level, have music playing as participants enter. Also, depending on the activity, play music throughout the workshop to enhance the mood. Keep in mind that for some activities, silence may be the best background music. iPods or MP3 players are the most convenient way to store and travel with your tunes. Plus, because of their light weight, you won't have to deal with all of today's airport safety issues.

◆ Play music during breaks and as participants are leaving the session.

◆ As you select music to play during your session, be sure to respect copyright laws. Restrict your selections to music that you have the copyright to. Many training supply companies offer music that you can purchase and play in a training session. Also, up-and-coming artists and vendors usually will give you permission to play their music without much problem (although they would probably appreciate an acknowledgment during your session).

◆ Have participants hum television theme songs, such as the one from the game show *Jeopardy,* during activities to speed things up.

Mistake #5:
Not generating spirit, color, or energy in the room

Jim's Gems:

◆ To create more ambiance and energy in your rooms, decorate the walls, chair backs, ceilings, and floors. Spirited room decor aids in the learning process. Remember when you were in first, second, and third grade?

◆ A nice way to welcome your partic-ipants is to write their names on the flipchart floor welcome mat.

◆ To encourage participant owner-ship, have the learners dress up their name tents. They can write questions, quotes, best ideas, and action items on them.

Prepare the room so that people feel your training style and your personal power.

◆ For the kinesthetic folks in the room, place tangible props such as Silly Putty, Koosh balls, or stress balls on the tables.

◆ Put quotations, important content, and other timely messages on the flipcharts around the room.

Mistake #6:
Failing to offer refreshments on the tables

Jim's Gem:

♦ To foster participation and encourage learning retention, put candy, water, mints, and so forth on the participants' tables.

Mistake #7:
Not providing reference material or special literature on the tables

Jim's Gems:

♦ To help participants locate various people in the organization, have a small organizational departmental directory on every table.

♦ To keep learners current with what's new in the industry, place industry readings and articles on the tables.

For motivational reading, put endorsement letters from previous participants on the tables.

♦ To help participants become more familiar with the organization's or external consultant's trainers, put their bios in the participant workbooks or on the tables.

♦ For additional reference reading, put a top-ten list of content-related information on the tables.

Mistake #8:
Having poor lighting in the room

Jim's Gems:

♦ Adjust the lighting to suit your workshop purposes. Get help from the facilities management staff or hotel team to assist you.

♦ If you are using PowerPoint slides or an overhead projector, make sure you know how to adjust the lights and draperies as needed.

♦ Don't keep the lights too dim for too long or your participants might grab a catnap!

♦ Keep in mind the participants' learning styles; some people might want enough light to take notes as you are showing PowerPoint slides.

Mistake #9:
Subjecting the learners to a room that's too hot or cold

Jim's Gem:

◆ Avoid freezer and sauna-like conditions by getting help from the facilities management staff or hotel team. Your learners will quickly let you know what the room temperature feels like. Don't ignore their pleas.

Mistake #10:
Failing to use the entire room during the workshop

Jim's Gems:

◆ To connect with your learners and enhance their experience, arrange the room so that you can use the back, the corners, and the front for activities.

◆ To avoid having a cluttered, sloppy room, remove any unnecessary charts, chairs, and tables from the room.

◆ To aid with accelerated and experiential learning and learning retention, create activities during which participants can sit, stand, change tables and seats, move to the corners, and present their ideas from various places in the room.

In the Trenches

I can recall the time where I spent two memorable days with one of my clients as I was facilitating our Total Awesome Trainer/Facilitator workshop. The weather was perfect. The location, southern California, was ideal. The participants were sensational. The food was delicious, and the hotel and staff were top notch.

The one pimple on my workshop face was the training room. Rather than a spacious room geared for interaction and experiential learning, the room felt as narrow as a conga line during a wedding reception in a tiny banquet room.

Throughout the two days, I felt as if I was training in a train car. It wasn't my client's mistake. It was mine. I had approved the room thinking that I could work around it. I had worked in smaller rooms before without a problem, but the goals for those workshops were different. I lost sight of the fact that I was about to lead a two-day train-the-trainer workshop. I needed a room where we could roam, practice, design, and experience high-energy activities.

I tried to mask my emotions by ignoring the room's dimensions, and although it appeared as though I did, I knew inside that I didn't. Whenever I wanted to walk to the back of the room, it was like getting up to go to the restroom in a crowded movie theater. I had to say, "Excuse me, pardon me, excuse me, pardon me," as I maneuvered through the participants. I adjusted many of the activities and exercises to suit our limitations. My movement was restricted, and I love to work a room as much as paparazzi like to take photos. From the placement of the projector, to the participant's large round tables (two on one side and one on the other), to my long props and supplies table, everything seemed *thistight*. Like a hangnail, I let the room's narrow size bother me.

The participants would tell you that they had a positive workshop experience. However, regarding my own personal power, I did not. On my plane ride home, I read the evaluations and they were sterling, but nearly every evaluation had comments about the room size and how they wished we would have had more space. Yes, the session proved to be productive, but I didn't feel like it was one of my typical, high-energy workshops. My experience helped pull it off. The session would have been even more productive if I had remembered the goals for my session and worked to get a larger room.

 **Building Your Action Plan:
Room Setup Mistakes**

My top three mistakes are:

1. _____

2. _____

3. _____

My action steps to correct these mistakes are:

1. _____

2. _____

3. _____

I'm committed to correcting these mistakes because:

_____

_____

_____

3

Audiovisual and Visual Aid Mistakes

What are pancakes without the syrup? Mashed potatoes without the gravy? Macaroni without the cheese? They're all familiar, family favorite meals that are taken to another level of culinary enjoyment once the accompaniments, seasoning, spices, and the like are added. Audiovisual (A/V) and visual aids are the accompaniments and seasonings for trainings and presentations. The key, as in food preparation, is to provide just enough of the accompaniments and seasoning to create the perfect taste. You wouldn't want the extras to negate the taste of the meal, and neither would you want an abundance of AV and visual aids to smother the workshop content.

A/V and visual aids have been used forever. When they are used appropriately, the workshop, speech, or presentation flows masterfully. The slides sing and the workbooks rock. All the materials complement each other, creating a masterpiece! When used inappropriately, though, the trainer or presenter ends up with a session that is as much fun for the participants as waiting hours for a delayed flight home at a crowded airport. Have you experienced PowerPoint overkill, also known as death by PowerPoint? I'm sure you've witnessed word wars; that is, PowerPoint slides that consist mostly of words with few or no pictures. And, have you seen the facilitator meltdown macarena—the dance that frustrated facilitators and presenters break into when their computer malfunctions and they can't go on with the workshop because their entire presentation is the slideshow?

Within this chapter, I highlight 17 of the top A/V and visual aid mistakes. I continue to be amazed by the number of violations I see, many of which are easily avoided. What's more, I cannot believe how many trainers rely so heavily on them. Sometimes, I wonder if they have a choice. When I contract with a client to provide a motivational address, one of their first questions is, "What are your A/V needs?" When I reply that I don't have any aside from a microphone and a sound system for music because I seldom use slides, they are astonished. They'll say, "Are you sure you don't have slides?" They seem to think that the quality of my presentation is going to be diminished because I'm not using slides. I have to remind them I incorporate other visual aids (namely, the audience and myself) into my presentation.

A/V and visual aids are just that—aids. They should add to the overall quality of your presentation and workshop materials. Read on to see what mistakes you're going to eliminate going forward.

Mistake #1:
Not having interactive elements embedded in your handouts

Jim's Gems:

- ◆ To support more individual handout responsibility and use, provide plenty of blank space in your handouts for note taking; put a creative graphic on the page to entice people to take notes.
- ◆ Provide a "best ideas," "top tips," or "action items" page for learners to record their most significant ideas.
- ◆ Provide blank lines for participants to write in correct answers, thereby imparting more energy to your lectures and avoiding the ho-hum lecture syndrome.
- ◆ To make the participant workbooks easier to navigate, suggest that the participants use self-stick page flags to label their most important pages; you can also use this approach as an opening activity by having them identify the pages they're looking forward to reviewing.

- Use the back sleeve of the binder (if possible) for participants to store their "top 10 takeaways" page; this is where they can write the ideas they plan to implement immediately back on the job.

Mistake #2:
Not testing your equipment or technology before the session

Jim's Gems:

- To avoid embarrassing workshop moments, spend some time becoming familiar with any technology you plan to use and do a practice run.
- Right before your presentation or workshop, preview your slides again to make sure there are no glitches.
- To avoid creating jarring loud noises and sounds, check the volume of your video, CD, or DVD player.

To make it easy for you to identify the appropriate switches when using unfamiliar equipment, place green (on), red (off), and blue (volume) dots on the most important operating switches.

- To avoid walking in front of the screen and bumping into the projector table, determine before your presentation how much walking-around space you have.
- Work with your microphone cord to see how much movement distance you have to ensure that you can move freely during your presentation.

Mistake #3:
Failing to cue your video to the appropriate spot

Jim's Gem:

- Fast-forward your video to the appropriate starting point to avoid the credits and seamlessly integrate the video content into your delivery.

Mistake #4:
Failing to adjust the volume to the appropriate level before the video or music begins

Jim's Gems:

◆ Have your video or audio volume cued accordingly. Blasting sounds at the outset will certainly drive your audience bonkers.

◆ Make sure that speakers, if available, are appropriately placed and that learners in all parts of the room will be able to hear.

Mistake #5:
Not having a projection screen of an appropriate size

Jim's Gems:

◆ For optimal viewing by the participants, the screen size you use should be 1 inch in width by 1 inch in length for every participant in the room. For example, if your audience includes 40 participants, your screen size should be 40 inches wide by 40 inches long. For extra large audiences, you may need several screens.

Also, position your screen in the far right corner (the facilitator's right side if he or she is standing in the front of the room), not in the center. If the screen is in the center of the room, facilitators often find themselves standing in front of the screen. For extra large audiences you may need several screens.

Mistake #6:
Using too many words on your slides

Jim's Gem:

◆ To enhance participant attention and learning retention, adhere to the six-by-six rule when you create your slides and flipcharts: no more than six words per line, six lines per slide or flipchart page.

Mistake #7:
Using PowerPoint slides that consist entirely of words

Jim's Gems:

♦ Use more pictures than words on your slides. A great majority (55 percent) of your participants are visual learners. Have you ever heard someone say, "Do you see what I'm saying?" Remember, a picture is worth a thousand words. So, add more pictures to your word-laden slides.

♦ Take advantage of PowerPoint's customization and animation features to make engaging slides, but don't overdo it. People get bored with words and graphic images flying on and off the screen with every single slide.

Mistake #8:
Not creating surprises or spontaneity with your visuals

Jim's Gems:

♦ To add more interest, intrigue, and fun to your workshops, create surprise elements to support your visuals. For example, tape index cards with questions, answers, or best practices written on them underneath your participants' chairs.

♦ Hang covered best practices flipcharts on ceilings. After you review a module, you can uncover the flipchart and segue to the next learning point.

Set up a participant Wall of Fame for your learners to induct various participants for their outstanding classroom contributions.

♦ Place a sealed envelope bearing the words "Please do not touch or open me until the trainer instructs you to" in the center of each table. Ignore the envelope during the session. If asked about it, just mention that at some point you will get to it. Wait until the end of the session to let them open it. Inside the envelope, provide a one-page handout with additional special learning points (or action plan sheets for them to complete).

- Leave some blank spaces on your wall charts; as an exercise, have participants fill them in during the session.
- Program a timer to go off every hour or so. When the bell rings, call on the person who raises his or her hand first. Award points or prizes for correct answers, and keep an ongoing score or tally.
- Use props from home to aid with action planning questions. For example, you could bring in an eggbeater and ask the participants how it might be related to dealing with change.
- Use the participants' names on your charts and slides. You could include your participants' names on the opening "welcome to the workshop" slide; create a welcome mat or high-five chart with everyone's name; place the mat on the floor or on a flipchart in the front of the room for participants to see as they enter and exit the room.

Mistake #9:
Using old/outdated resources or information

Jim's Gem:

- To maintain your credibility, keep updating your resources; check current industry publications, newsletters, magazines, and websites. Read books, watch videos, and listen to tapes that provide you with current trends and statistics.

Mistake #10:
Using unprofessional body language

Jim's Gems:

- View videotapes of yourself presenting while watching with a critical eye. What could you do to improve? Consider joining Toastmasters International so that you get additional opportunities to practice public speaking and obtain feedback from others.

Keep your shoes on, and do not slip your heel
out of the back of your shoe.

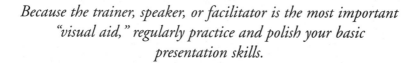

Because the trainer, speaker, or facilitator is the most important "visual aid," regularly practice and polish your basic presentation skills.

- Maintain great posture and superior eye communication while presenting.
- Avoid fidgeting with your jewelry or putting your hand in your pocket.
- Walk in an arc while presenting from the front of the room.
- Look confident and assured.
- Don't adjust or fix your underclothing while presenting or talking.

Mistake #11:
Not using participants or even yourself as a visual aid

Jim's Gems:
- To avoid solely relying on A/V or visual aids, get the participants involved in your demonstrations, stories, and illustrations. These will also keep your learners engaged.
- Depending on the learning activity or example, move your participants around the room. Use this approach when reviewing best practices and action ideas.
- To aid with learning retention and participant engagement, use a bit of theater (drama or acting) during your demonstrations and examples to drive home important points.

Mistake #12:
Using incorrect colors on flipcharts

Jim's Gem:
- For better readability, use dark colors (blacks, blues, greens, browns, purples) when writing words on the flipchart or on overhead transparencies. Use pastel colors (red, orange, yellow, pink) for highlighting.

Mistake #13:
Failing to bring all of your supplies to the session

Jim's Gem:

◆ To avoid having to rely on others (including your organization and the hotel staff) to deliver what you forgot, make a travel supply and tool kit. In your kit include professional and personal training musts such as Mr. Sketch markers, masking tape, Koosh balls or other throw toys, dice, extension cord, surge protector, page flags, index cards, envelopes, staple remover, scissors, Post-it notes, smiley-face page dots, rubber bands, push pins, blank sheets of paper, CDs, handkerchief, aspirin, breath mints, adhesive bandages, and a pocket mirror.

Mistake #14:
Continually walking in front of the screen

Jim's Gems:

◆ Be mindful about where you are standing when you're making a presentation by projecting slides or a video. Do not walk or stand in front of the screen when the projector is on. When you're using PowerPoint, you can blank the screen by pressing the appropriate button on your remote slide advancer, by hitting the B key on your keypad, or by turning the projector off. You could also present from either side of the projector or screen.

To avoid having to walk near the screen to the keyboard to advance your slides, use a remote slide advancer.

Mistake #15:
Using visuals, slides, or graphics that are too small or hard to see

Jim's Gem:

◆ To avoid frustrating your learners, use at least a 24-point font for your PowerPoint slides. If you ever have to apologize for your type size, graphics, charts, or pictures being too small or difficult to read, then they are. Don't use them again. Have more consideration for your participants.

Mistake #16:
Not giving a learning or feedback assignment prior to showing a video

Jim's Gems:

- ◆ To stimulate more participant dialog after showing a video, give your participants an assignment or something to look for during the video (for example, benefits, features, mistakes, best practices). After the video, ask participants to share their thoughts relative to their assignment.

- ◆ Before showing the video, divide the room in half. Give the two groups different questions to address or different things to look for in the video. Afterward, the two groups can report back on what they learned. For example, one side of the room could look for benefits while the other half looks for features.

Mistake #17:
Using a lavaliere microphone for a keynote address

Jim's Gem:

- ◆ Use a handheld microphone when delivering a keynote address. You're able to use more voice inflection and variety by moving the handheld microphone closer to or away from your mouth. A lavaliere microphone remains stationary, making it difficult for you to vary your voice to the same extent.

In the Trenches

Devin was on a roll. The workshop was going superbly although he wasn't surprised because it was a session he had facilitated numerous times.

His decision to abandon his typical one-hour prep time routine didn't seem to hurt either as he glided, Michelle Kwan-like, through the material. He figured that showing up just 20 minutes before the session would still leave him plenty of time because all he had to do was hang up a few flipcharts, prepare the slideshow and projector, and distribute the participant manuals.

With his enthusiasm building after every successful module, Devin had the group eating out of the palm of his hand. What made his day seem even more rewarding was that several managers were in attendance, previewing the session to see if they would send their staff members.

With a half hour to go before lunch, Devin readied the group for their final activity before the break. He introduced the video, then moved toward the video player to turn it on. Devin pressed play, but nothing happened. He checked the power cords on the television and on the player. They were both plugged in. He checked the power buttons, and they were turned on as well. Embarrassed silence engulfed the room as he worked feverishly to right this problem. "Maybe the tape is not in there," one of the participants called out. With a sheepish grin adorning his face, Devin looked on his materials table and located the video. After a brief apology, he pushed the video into the slot and pressed "play."

Everyone immediately covered their ears and took cover as the volume on the television set was up to about 75 decibels. To make matters worse, Devin had not set the video to the starting spot. Closing credits and triumphant theme music filled the room. Realizing that things were starting to get away from him, Devin put an abrupt halt to the debacle by turning off the television and stopping the video player. Frustration blanketed his face as he waited a lonnnnnnnng minute for the video to rewind. Devin stood to the side, offered a little small talk, turned on the television, turned down the volume, and then pressed the play button on the VCR. Opening credits greeted the group this time but minus the loud volume.

Realizing that he should just leave well enough alone, he let the video continue, credits and all. Twenty minutes later, the video ended and Devin dismissed the group for lunch without a video debrief.

Building Your Action Plan:
Audiovisual and Visual Aid Mistakes

My top three mistakes are:

1. _____

2. _____

3. _____

My action steps to correct these mistakes are:

1. _____

2. _____

3. _____

I'm committed to correcting these mistakes because:

_____

_____

_____

4

Motivation Mistakes

Participant motivation plays a significant role in the outcome of any session. Speakers and facilitators can move through their sessions with greater ease once they realize that providing solid content is not merely enough to motivate the audience. It's imperative that trainers create an environment where learners want to explore, interact, and participate. As soon as the participants enter the room, they should know that this is a special place.

Although each person is responsible for his or her level of motivation, the facilitator's job is enormous. Throughout the session, he or she must discover what's important to each person and continue to tap into that motivational factor. To do this, trainers must use a variety of facilitation methods and adult learning, participant-driven techniques. And, they must adopt different roles—coach, psychologist, cheerleader, drill sergeant, and mentor—to help learners maintain and increase their motivation.

Trainers, at times, miss the motivation mark by not being flexible and continuing to use the same approach, even if it's failing. They ignore the significance of group interaction and don't place enough value on warming up the audience. Putting participants on the spot and criticizing them for incorrect answers kill motivation as well.

Ultimately, numerous factors go into the motivation equation. By doing something as simple as individually greeting the participants as they walk in the room or fostering friendly competition, the trainer is the conductor who, if skillful and discerning, can bring out the best in his or her participants.

This chapter covers 21 of the most prevalent trainer motivation mistakes. Let's take a look at the many little things that can determine whether a learner soars or snores.

Mistake #1:
Putting participants on the spot

Jim's Gems:

♦ To avoid completely losing your learners, be tuned into their looks, facial expressions, and energy level.

♦ Know what your goal is before calling on someone to avoid falling prey to personal agendas.

To avoid catching people off guard, call their name first before asking the question.

♦ Spread your questions around. Get everyone involved.

♦ Take a "temperature check" during the break. Ask individuals who have not contributed what needs to happen for them to participate more fully.

♦ To get more participation from the entire group, call on table groups to provide answers, not just individuals.

Mistake #2:
Announcing at the session's outset that there is going to be a test

Jim's Gems:

♦ To avoid stressing out your group and creating unnecessary tension in the room, remind the group at the end of the previous day's session that there will be a test the next day. Begin that day's workshop by reviewing the previous day's materials. Then introduce the test. Do not introduce the test first. If possible, use other words when discussing the test (e.g., a way for us to measure your understanding of the material).

◆ When facilitating the pretest discussion, ask the group what additional information they need to do well on the test. List their answers, and then tell them you will be focusing on their concern areas as you prepare them for the test (that day or the next).

Mistake #3:
Failing to welcome each participant personally as he or she enters the room for the first time

Jim's Gems:

◆ To establish a warm and hearty environment, meet and greet participants as they enter the room. Create small talk by thanking them for attending and by asking them what they hope to obtain from the session. You can use information you receive to help create more personal and individualized introductions.

◆ Once participants take their seats and before the session begins, go over and visit with them. Introduce yourself and take note of their goals and expectations.

◆ While making your way around the room initially, let each person know that he or she is in for a powerful experience; tell each person that the timing is perfect for him or her to be there.

Mistake #4:
Failing to build curiosity or intrigue into the material

Jim's Gems:

◆ Leave a blank line in the middle of the list of the prepared objectives and agenda items. Tell the group it's a mystery objective.

◆ Build in intrigue by not telling them everything about how the day is going to unfold. Add question marks to the agenda.

Arrange for a mystery guest speaker to come in, perhaps a manager, a previous workshop participant, or an executive.

Mistake #5:
Setting workshop ground rules or learning rules for the participants

Jim's Gem:

◆ To encourage personal accountability and responsibility, put participants in teams to develop the workshop ground rules or learning rules regarding confidentiality, participation, and so forth. Give the group approximately two minutes to do this, and then record their answers on the flipchart. Add a couple of your rules to flesh out the list. In most cases, 90 percent of what they develop are rules that would be on your list. In all likelihood, you will have an easier time getting them to follow and police their ground rules than yours.

Mistake #6:
Telling the group that they will be getting out early but not being able to fulfill that promise

Jim's Gem:

◆ To avoid having frustrated and disappointed learners, never tell your group that you're going to end the session early. If you're ahead of schedule, keep it to yourself until the end and surprise them with an early departure. If someone asks you what time the session is supposed to end, always stick to the time originally listed on the invitation.

Mistake #7:
Using too many activities

Jim's Gems:

◆ Participants need time to process and absorb your information. You can wear them out with too many activities. One or two activities every hour should be sufficient.

Remember, too much of anything is too much. Maintain a healthy balance of lecture, group activity, partner work, and individual work.

◆ Vary the kinds of activities you use. Provide low-, medium-, and high-risk activities. Nevertheless, use them in moderation.

◆ To help with retention and application of the participants' new knowledge or skills, provide crucial debrief and note-taking time after an activity.

Mistake #8:
Not creating small group work opportunities

Jim's Gems:

◆ To appeal to the variety of learning styles in the room, alternate between small group and large group activities. Have participants work in pairs, threes, and fours. Avoid creating groups over six unless you develop groups within groups; if the initial group has more than six people, participants may drift, disengage, or contribute little to the task. Also, provide opportunities for learners to work individually.

◆ Solving case studies, developing an action plan list, creating a best practices list, developing a presentation, and reviewing content are all great opportunities for small group activities.

Mistake #9:
Moving too quickly through the information or not allowing adequate process or note-taking time

Jim's Gems:

◆ To help with retention and engagement, teach in chunks. Your process should include disseminating information (the lecture), letting the participants "marinate" in it or discuss it among themselves for a while, then reviewing it. Alternate review activities and review length.

To make sure that you're not moving too quickly, keep asking yourself, "How do I know they know?" Use a variety of approaches to keep checking in.

◆ To leverage the learning, provide high-energy content reviews after long presentations by guest speakers.

◆ Ask your guest speakers to build in review or process time during their presentations to ensure proper understanding.

Mistake #10:
Failing to use the participant's name tents as learning aids

Jim's Gems:

◆ To take advantage of an underused motivational tool, have the participants use their name tents (primarily the back) to record learning goals, difficult questions, motivational quotations, participation commitments, and best practices.

◆ On the back of their name tents, have participants record what they are going to do to get the most from the learning experience and what they want the facilitator to do to help support their goal.

◆ Have participants stand their name tents vertically to signal to you when they have finished an activity.

Mistake #11:
Not allowing for friendly, professional competition

Jim's Gems:

◆ To keep your sessions lively and engaging, incorporate fun, quick, content-related competitive activities during your sessions.

◆ Have participants compete from their seats or use the entire room to foster high-energy interaction.

◆ Competitive activities that consistently work include versions of television shows such as *Family Feud, Jeopardy, The Price Is Right, Name That Tune, Wheel of Fortune, What's My Line?, Survivor,* and *Pardon the Interruption* or games such as relay races, hot potato, bingo, scavenger hunt, Pictionary, and Outburst.

◆ Create competition with role plays by assigning points for accuracy,

For smaller groups, have participants compete against time or their previous top score.

thoroughness, comprehensiveness, creativity, and the "wow!" factor (something that is totally out of the box).

◆ Have participants work in pairs to compete against their peers.

◆ Use trivia questions and brainteasers. *USA Today* is a great, inexpensive resource for contemporary trivia.

Mistake #12:
Forgetting to provide freedom and safety in the room

Jim's Gems:

◆ To help with participation and morale, remind your learners at the outset that this is a safe environment and provide examples of what happens in a safe environment.

◆ Share with them examples of what could happen to the workshop if they did not adhere to the ground rules or learning rules.

◆ Post your ground or learning rules in a prominent place (under a wall clock, for example) for all to see throughout the day.

◆ Ask for volunteers from each table to help enforce the ground or learning rules.

Post quotations on the walls to highlight the value of participation freedom and safety.

◆ Make it a point to get around to each participant to check in and determine what he or she needs to encourage complete participation.

Mistake #13:
Not calling participants by name during the session

Jim's Gems:

◆ To better connect with your learners, use creative activities and methods to remember their names. For example, write their names next to their learning goals on a flipchart page and post it on the wall; have them write an adjective in front on their name on their name tent that describes their work style, noting that the adjective must begin with the same first letter of their first name (Careful Connie, for example); or have them create individual flipchart sheets on which they write their name and three workshop wishes.

◆ Simply take a peek at their name tents when you call on them.
◆ Take time during the break to get to know each participant.
◆ During the introduction, ask participants what they would like to be called during the session. Have fun with this, but don't let it get out of hand.
◆ During the break, go around to each name tent and attempt to visualize the person in that seat.

Mistake #14:
Not appearing excited or passionate about your subject matter

Jim's Gems:

Make sure that your facial expressions are congruent with your words.

◆ To build stronger connections and to motivate your audience, appear enthusiastic and inspired as you review the course objectives.
◆ Smile and engage in small talk during the participant introductions.
◆ Be open and inviting—and show it!
◆ Believe in your content.

Mistake #15:
Saying "Let's review," or "Are there any questions?"

Jim's Gems:

◆ To generate more questions, alter your language when asking for questions. Instead of asking, "Are there any questions?" try, "What are your questions?" or "Who has a burning question that they've been sitting on?
◆ Ask team tables to develop questions.
◆ Facilitate sneaky review activities—brief, fun activities whereby learners review content without readily realizing that they're reviewing the content.
◆ Have participants develop questions for each other or set up a contest with participants forming questions to stump each other.
◆ Move into the review without announcing it.

Mistake #16:
Failing to get participants up and moving

Jim's Gems:

- To stimulate more learner energy and engagement, get participants up early in the workshop and keep them moving throughout the day.
- Create opportunities for them to move when doing partner work, small group work, and large group work.
- Use participants as flipchart recorders.
- Use a best-ideas flipchart for participants to post their key take aways during the workshop.
- Use a "things-that-make-you-go-hmmmm" flipchart for participants to post their questions during the workshop.
- When participants return from the break, have a high-energy review assignment that requires them to move around the room.
- When participants finish a task, have them stand and then share their results with another person.

Change the learning venue by allowing participants to leave the room during certain activities.

- Use activities or games such as *Family Feud,* scavenger hunt, case study challenges, or Pictionary to highlight key learning points.

Mistake #17:
Not connecting with each person

Jim's Gems:

- Introduce yourself to each participant as he or she enters the room.
- During breaks, go over to the learners who remain in the room and discuss the workshop and their personal learning goals.

Maintain great eye communication.

- Use their names during the session.
- Use their names and their learning goals when referring to content that relates to their goals.
- Smile more. Make it a genuine one.

- With regard to eye communication, remember to use the "single thought, one person" (STOP) method when reviewing information. As you express a thought, look at one particular person, then move on.
- Be real, genuine, and humble. Avoid "egonomics," that is, condescending, know-it-all behavior.

Mistake #18:
Not challenging participants to stretch and reach new behavioral heights

Jim's Gems:

- To give participants time to discover and to form answers, avoid answering questions as soon as you ask them. Give learners time to consider the question.

During review moments, ask your learners, "What are you going to do that you haven't already done?"

- Challenge learners to come up with multiple answers. Don't always settle on the first answer.
- Create content discussion situations for participants to challenge each other.
- Use language that reinforces the notion that there is room for growth.
- During feedback moments, be sincere and candid. Give constructive feedback as well as positive feedback.

Call the constructive feedback "polish." Don't be afraid to offer specifics about what the learner has to do to improve.

- Use probing when questioning your group.
- Ask application questions. Here's an example: "How are you going to apply what you've learned today back at work?"

Mistake #19:
Not creating opportunities for participants to take personal responsibility and accountability for the session's learning objectives, expectations, and outcomes

Jim's Gems:

- Have participants develop the session's ground/learning rules.

- Allow participants to assess how much they currently know about the learning objectives at the beginning of the session.
- Offer an opportunity for partici- pants to speak about what they'd like to learn during the day.
- Have participants share what they're going to do to ensure that their learning objectives come to fruition.

Encourage participants to note when their key learning objective has been met and how they are going to incorporate it going forward.

- Encourage participants to facilitate and comment on teach-backs.
- Let participants play a role in determining the length of the break.
- Have participants handle other participants' difficult behavior.
- Let them participate in the closing activities and comments.
- Have participants share how they plan to support each other during the workshop.

Mistake #20:
Letting people know that the upcoming dry information is going to be dry

Jim's Gems:
- Believe in your content.

To avoid creating disinterested learners, refrain from making comments that provide a negative preview of what's about to occur.

Mistake #21:
Not giving participants choices

Jim's Gems:
- To encourage individual ownership, don't do everything for your participants; rather, ask them what they would like to do. ("Would you like another example?" "Would you like to move right in to the activity?")

- ◆ If possible, let your participants have a say in which learning objective they would like to review next.
- ◆ Remind participants throughout the day that they play a key role in the session's outcome.
- ◆ Let participants play a role in determining when or if they need a break and how long the break should be. For example, you could have someone roll two or three foam dice to determine the duration of the break.

In the Trenches

Terry was a pharmaceutical sales trainer. He had attended a one-day version of my train-the-trainer workshop, and now I was going to have the opportunity to observe him at his organization facilitating one of his new-hire sales training classes. I was thrilled to be there because I take pleasure in seeing students immediately incorporate what they've learned back on the job, where the stakes are higher. Two months had gone by since Terry had attended the session; yet, I expected great things from him. His energy, humor, creativity, and approach to how adults learn were session highlights.

I took my seat in the back of the room, prepared to fill up my notepad with positive feedback. The room quickly filled up with young, raring-to-go, hearty new hires. I immediately thought to myself that Terry was going to have his hands full, but with what I saw in him during our workshop, he could easily pull it off. Salespeople can be spirited and even demanding at times, but I doubted he would have a problem. He was equipped with many new tools, and he was probably anxious to use them for the first time.

During his introductory remarks, I almost fell off my chair! The amiable, charismatic trainer that I had come to know turned into a belligerent, taskmaster right before my very eyes. His welcoming words turned into a laundry list of what would and what would not be tolerated during their three weeks of training. The participants began looking at each other with "Is this guy for real?" stares, and I was with them. I wished I could call a timeout, but Terry and I had agreed beforehand that I would not interrupt.

When he put them into their first activity, I motioned for him to join me in the back of the room. "Terry, what are you doing?" I asked. "You shouldn't treat your folks that way." "Jim, you have to jump on these new hires right away and let them know who's boss," he said. "If you give them an inch, they'll take over the class, Jim. You have to set the tone immediately." I was stunned.

Terry returned to his throne in the front of the room and proceeded to violate every rule of participant motivation. He criticized them for incorrect answers, talked down to them in a strong paternal voice, yelled at them when it was time to bring them back together after an activity, told them to really pay attention as he reviewed the "dry material" (his words), and used threats to get them back on time from the break.

Astonished, I saw what was once an energetic, lively group of new hires turn into a quiet, subdued group of note-takers. And, that's what they did for the most part all day as he lectured and showed slides for nearly two-thirds of the session. I met Terry at the end of the workshop to offer some feedback. My earlier attempt had been met with a quick brush-off, "Jim, I'm pretty tied up right now. Can we talk later?"

Before I could share my thoughts, Terry fired first with, "I know you're going to say that I was too tough on these guys, but you have to understand, I have them for three weeks and I have to establish control right away. If I don't, they'll take over the class. That touchy-feely stuff you teach is good for some classes, but I think my way is more effective for sessions like this."

I shared my disappointment about his facilitation decorum and style and his view on adult learning. I offered several pages of candid feedback on what he could have done to achieve better results. Nevertheless, Terry was not budging. My Motivational Matt had turned into Terry the Terrible, and he was not going to change. I hope what I later shared with his manager contributed to some evolution.

Building Your Action Plan:
Motivation Mistakes

My top three mistakes are:

1. _____

2. _____

3. _____

My action steps to correct these mistakes are:

1. _____

2. _____

3. _____

I'm committed to correcting these mistakes because:

_____

_____

_____

5

Difficult Participant Mistakes

Managing challenging participant behavior requires patience, discernment, guile, perseverance, skill, and a healthy dose of luck. The behavior can come at you head on or catch you off guard. The behavior can come from the quietest person in the room who has not contributed anything or from the manager who had promised to come and just observe. And, just when you think you've seen it all, a new challenging behavior is staring you in the eyes. Ultimately, the facilitator's or trainer's reaction is the key because it's not what happens to you that counts, it's how you handle it.

Over the years, trainers have coined some names for many of the difficult participants they've faced; for example, the latecomer, the big mouth, the know-it-all, the debater, the side conversationalist, the prisoner, the vacationer, the saboteur, the sage, the sleeper, the introvert, and the confronter. Their sole mission, some maintain, is to cause the trainer grief and raise havoc. Some trainers joke that there must be a DPU (Difficult Participant University) out there that provides tips and techniques to sharpen their challenging behavior skill set. Based on my observations, however, trainers and speakers also play a role in stirring the challenging behavior pot. Not responding or responding incorrectly can really exacerbate the behavior. That's primarily what this chapter is about. Fourteen of the most common mistakes we make when dealing with difficult participants are highlighted.

Pay special attention to Jim's Gems and determine if there are adjustments you can make to your delivery. A tweak here and a mind shift there could pay off in a significant way. We've all been difficult participants at some point. What brought us around? Once you recognize the influence of adult learning principles, the power you have, and how to use the group as an ally, you're well on your way to dealing effectively with difficult participants.

Mistake #1:
Ignoring the difficult or challenging behavior

Jim's Gems:

◆ To keep the behavior from brewing, confront the person and ask if there is anything you could do to help.

◆ Use direct methods to silence the behavior. For example, refer to the ground rules that the participants helped to establish; inform the learners that that behavior will not be accepted; have a coaching moment with the person during the break to inform him or her of what will happen if the behavior continues; ask the perpetrator to share what his or her goal is for behaving in that fashion.

◆ Walk or move closer to the person and facilitate from that area.

Mistake #2:
Letting the big mouth or the overzealous participant go on and on

Jim's Gems:

◆ To gain allies and sample multiple viewpoints, ask others for their opinions regarding the topic.

◆ Tell the group that this question is for those who have not shared much up to that point or say that you'd like to hear from someone at a particular table.

◆ To silence big mouths temporarily, tell them that they have contributed plenty up to this point, acknowledge their contributions, and say that you're going to put them on the bench for now because you want to hear from others. Warn them that you want them to stay ready because you're going to need their contributions at some point.

- When they stop talking for a moment, exploit their pauses. They'll pause for a moment if you say their name.
- Limit their sharing by distributing participation chips. Each person gets three or any number you deem appropriate. Every time a person contributes, he or she has to sur-

Give the big mouth an assignment that does not require talking, such as serving as scribe for the group.

render a chip. When the big mouth runs out of chips, that ends his or her participation until you distribute more chips. They cannot take chips from their teammates.

Mistake #3:
Ignoring latecomers who *unintentionally* arrive late

Jim's Gems:

- To put latecomers at ease, welcome them and invite them to take a seat. Provide a short overview of what's been discussed up to that point.
- Thank them for coming and assign a buddy to help them catch up with the material during the next break.
- Check in with them during the break to see if everything is OK.

Mistake #4:
Ignoring latecomers who *intentionally* arrive late

Jim's Gem

- Start on time. When people arrive late on purpose, perhaps dawdling outside the room, you should stop facilitating as they take their seat (you don't want to keep presenting during a distraction), welcome them, and wait for them to sit down. Check in with them during the break, and empower them to connect with someone to bring them up to speed. If they are late after the break, have them share in front of the group three things they learned so far during the workshop or have them share one thing for every minute they are late. Be consistent in the way you handle these difficult participants.

Mistake #5:
Debating with the debater

Jim's Gems:

- ◆ To avoid getting pulled in, don't lose sight of the rest of the group. Address the debater's challenge, but bring others into the discussion.
- ◆ Tell the debater that you will speak to him or her in greater detail during the break.
- ◆ During your classroom discussion, make sure to ask him or her

To shift the focus from the debater and to redirect your energy, move away from the debater when presenting. Use welcoming gestures to bring others into the conversation. Specifically ask others if they felt the same way or what they would do differently.

what the goal is, relative to the point he or she is attempting to make.
- ◆ During your classroom discussion, make sure to ask debaters what needs to happen for them to feel as though their point has been made.

Mistake #6:
Spending too much classroom time with the know-it-all

Jim's Gems:

- ◆ To massage their insecurity and ego, acknowledge their expertise and ask them to be ready to share their experience when called upon.
- ◆ To take advantage of their expertise and to give them an opportunity to mentor others, pair them up with less experienced participants.
- ◆ During breaks, give them challenging, content-related brainteasers.
- ◆ To see if they really want to demonstrate their subject matter expertise, offer them designated time (no more than five minutes) to present.

To get them to think that they're contributing to the session's outcome, ask them to provide one final example after you've already fielded several answers from the group.

- Appeal to their ego by saying that you welcome having experienced people, such as them, in the session.
- Avoid getting caught in lengthy one-on-one debates or conversations.
- Encourage and welcome other viewpoints. Don't let know-it-alls think they have the upper hand or that they're getting to you.
- When they stop talking, exploit their pauses.
- Ask them to help with evaluating and scoring during role plays and participant presentations.

Mistake #7:
Raising your voice, in parental fashion, to quiet a loud group

Jim's Gems:
- To avoid treating your learners like children, develop a signal that you will use to quiet the group. While establishing the ground rules or before an activity, let the group know what the signal is (for example, snapping your fingers, clapping your hands, raising your hands above your head, hitting a chime).
- Partner with volunteers from each table to help quiet the group. Tell them what your signal is, and inform them that their task is to help you quiet the group by getting their table to quiet down when you give the signal.
- To avoid creating a hostile environment, be firm but refrain from raising your voice or yelling at the group to get their attention.
- To allow the participants to feel your energy and hear your voice more clearly, move into the middle of the group when attempting to get them to settle down.
- Offer rewards in the form of points, for example, for the first group to settle down and return to their seats after the activity.
- See mistake #13 in chapter 1 for more ideas.

Mistake #8:
Allowing cell phones, pagers, Blackberry devices, and other participant technology to take over the session

Jim's Gems:

◆ To avoid disruptions, have participants turn their cell phones and pagers to vibrate or, better yet, to off.

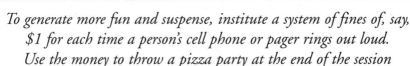

To generate more fun and suspense, institute a system of fines of, say, $1 for each time a person's cell phone or pager rings out loud. Use the money to throw a pizza party at the end of the session or to buy workshop supplies.

◆ Be firm when informing the group that you will not let cell phones and other technology become a distraction.
◆ When someone's phone rings, walk over and ask to answer the call for them. Tell the caller that the person is not available and that he or she will call back after the session is over.

Mistake #9:
Allowing the "prisoner" (a person who doesn't want to be at the session or the person whom management has sent for a particular reason) to imprison others

Jim's Gems:

◆ To stop the toxic behavior from filling the room, confront the prisoner early and find out why he or she does not want to be there.

Tell a story about a time when you were a prisoner and how the trainer helped to shift your mindset to a more positive place.

◆ Meet with the prisoner, one on one, during the break. Share with him or her the behavior you'd like to see and what the consequences will be for not meeting your expectations.
◆ Spend time at the outset finding out why some folks are disgruntled. Make a list, using their comments, about

why (in their opinion) they *shouldn't* be at the session. Then, immediately make a list, using the other participants' comments and yours about why they *should* be at the workshop. Inform the entire group that you appreciate both perspectives and you will work very hard to create an environment where everyone leans to the positive side of the chart before the session is over. Also say, for those who cannot shake their prisoner perspective, that you would like to meet with them following the session to work with them and their managers regarding what could be done to help shift their focus.

◆ If the prisoner's behavior becomes too disruptive, dismiss him or her at the next break or take an unplanned break to handle the dismissal.

◆ When dealing with the prisoner, focus on the behavior not the person. Your goal should be to get the challenging behavior to stop.

Mistake #10:
Allowing the "vacationer"—a person who just wants to relax and take it easy during the session—to take a vacation

Jim's Gems:

◆ Balance the lecture with interactive exercises.

◆ Create friendly competition early in the session.

◆ Hone in on getting vacationers to share their learning goals and what they are going to do to achieve them. Then, share what you're going to do to help them reach the goals.

◆ Keep switching people among the table groups.

To get the vacationers involved, put them to work early and often. Have them be a scribe, materials manager (the person who distributes supplies), spokesperson, or team leader.

Mistake #11:
Letting the socializer socialize

Jim's Gems:

- To acknowledge right away that their behavior will not be accepted, call them on their socializing.
- If their socializing becomes a distraction, meet with them one on one during the break.
- During the ground rule discussion, stress that there will be time for group interaction as well as individual work.
- To help them feel your power and energy, move closer or walk over to them during one of their socializing moments.

Highlight, somewhat in tongue-in-cheek fashion, the top two or three behaviors that can derail a workshop and why you don't permit those behaviors during your sessions. Mention that among such behaviors are oversocializing and side conversations.

- During your one-on-one discussion at the break, develop a signal for you to use when you think he or she is socializing too much. Also, state that you will dismiss him or her from the session if the behavior continues. Inform the socializer that you will be following up with management to explain his or her early departure.
- See also mistake #9 in this chapter.

Mistake #12:
Letting the manager or leader take over the class

Jim's Gems:

- To avoid surprises, connect with the manager beforehand, if possible, and discuss the role—observer, participant, question-and-answer leader during the break—that you would like him or her to play. This is especially important if he or she asks, "What role would you like me to play?"

To improve the communication between the two of you, set up a signal, such as when you stand, when you walk to the front of the room, or when you raise your hand, for turning the session back over to you.

◆ If you don't have the opportunity to meet with the manager beforehand, give him or her a task as soon as he or she enters the room: "Hi Maria, I'm glad that you could join us. Right before we go to our break, I'd like you to field a few questions. Thanks!"

◆ When you do give the manager the microphone or give the manager an opportunity to present, always set a time limit. Hint: Because executive types tend to double whatever time you give them, if you want managers to speak for 10 minutes, then tell them that they have five minutes.

◆ Meet with the manager one on one during the break if his or her behavior becomes overbearing or disruptive. During the meeting, stand firm and explain your perspective about what's happening. A manager's disruptive behavior could shut down learner participation. Get him or her to commit to changing such behavior.

◆ To encourage greater buy-in, ask managers to provide some assistance in helping you tailor your workshops to meet their needs. Get their input for what they think productive behavior from their workers should look like.

◆ Develop together a plan, script, or routine for their visits and participation. Get to know each other's workshop goals and facilitation styles.

Mistake #13:
Not knowing when and how to jump in to end a classroom debate

Jim's Gems:
◆ Interrupt the debate if it appears to be getting too heated or if there are a number of pauses before people respond.

Interject when the debate is at its highest point. It's best to have the participants thinking that they want more rather than that they've had too much.

- ◆ Break into the debate by thanking the group for being so passionate about the topic and suggesting that they maintain that passion throughout the day.
- ◆ Jump in if it appears that someone is getting frustrated, attacked, anxious, or becoming annoyed.
- ◆ To bring the debate slowly to a close, give the group a time limit, perhaps two more minutes, for continuing the debate.
- ◆ Facilitate or manage the debate by giving each person an opportunity to respond.

Mistake #14:
Not allowing the difficult participant to save face

Jim's Gems:

- ◆ Ask difficult participants what needs to happen during the session for them to feel heard, understood, and valued.
- ◆ Share with the group an experience when you demonstrated the same difficult behavior, why you did, and how you came around.

Thank the difficult participant for being so passionate about the subject matter.

- ◆ Thank the difficult participant for having the courage to say the unsaid.
- ◆ Thank the difficult participant for playing the devil's advocate role.
- ◆ Speak with the difficult participant during the break. Say that your goal is to create a safe environment for everyone, including him or her. Also, explain that you'd like the difficult behavior to stop and that you'd like to do some group problem solving around the dilemma when the session resumes.

In the Trenches

I had heard about Zoon before a Valuing Diversity workshop. His leadership team warned me that he was quite the character and that I might have my hands full. Never one to shun a challenge, I was actually eagerly anticipating my rendezvous with Zoon—at least that's what I thought.

It was the winter of 1991 when I was asked to facilitate the special diversity session for the organization's third-shift letter shop, which was responsible for printing, preparing, and mailing direct-mail materials. The thought of facilitating a workshop from 11:00 p.m. to 7:00 a.m. became more disconcerting to me than dealing with a participant who had too much pop in his tart. At that time our organization was well into its diversity initiative and I headed up the group office's diversity council. I was also one of the few trainers certified to deliver the program. Confidence was my best friend.

Sad to say, in my mind at that time, I believed that I was "the man" and no participant was going to turn any workshop, particularly a diversity workshop that I was leading, into a Ringling Brothers circus. I had seen plenty in my years as a trainer and I believed that I had been coached by the best. "Bring it on, Zoon," I thought as I drove up to the building at 10:00 p.m.

A dark parking lot at a campus that I was not too familiar with did not dampen my spirits or slow my groove as I pulled up to the building. I was on a mission. I was going to deliver an outstanding session and, in the process, take the gleam from Zoon's disruptive steam. He would be another trophy on my training mantel.

As I was putting the finishing touches on the room setup, participants started to walk in. Of course, I was looking for Zoon. Because no one gave me an exact description, I peered at every guy thinking he might be Zoon. I asked participants to put their names on their name tents, something that I generally would do during an opening icebreaker activity (not simply while they were waiting); however, I was eager to find out who this Zoon dude was. No luck. The name Zoon was not scribed on any of the name tents. Maybe he decided to blow off the class.

As soon as I started the introductions, Zoon, with a woman on each arm, walked in the room. The class started laughing, but not me. "It's on now," I thought. "Time to roll up my sleeves."

When it was his turn, Zoon, who was wearing sunglasses and a hat turned to the side, introduced himself, wrote "Z" on his name tent, and provided a glimpse into what was in store for me. The slender, 5-foot, 6-inch letter-shop professional looked nothing like I thought he would. I had expected George Foreman and I got Sammy Davis, Jr. (without the tuxedo, coiffed hair, cigarette, charisma, martini, and bling-bling). During his opening remarks, when I commented on the two female co-workers who accompanied him into the room, he offered that women could only make his food, make his bed, and make his babies. Incensed (but trying not to show it) by his comment and by the two women colluding with his obnoxious behavior, I made up my mind that I was going to give him some diversity medicine regardless of whether he liked it. I was going to put him over my diversity-trainer knee and spank the insanity out of him with my diversity belt.

That opening quip was not his only one. During the next eight hours he talked about everything. From politics to race relations, class issues to health care, his distorted views were voiced for the entire room to hear or challenge. I became his only challenger. He highlighted his appreciation and admiration for segregation, sexism, and the like. Everything that I said was met with a satirical, counter-opinion. It was as if none of the other 20 participants were in the room. Zoon and I were going toe to toe in Ali-Frazier style. I didn't see anyone raise his or her hand. My complete focus was on the out-of-control antagonist.

When the session ended, Zoon with his entourage in tow, winked at me and said, "I got you," as he walked to the door. He sure did. The other participants complained to management and rightly so. I eventually ran the session again with the same group, minus Zoon. The session went flawlessly. Nevertheless, from that point forward, I learned never to totally focus on one person and not try to "fix" anyone.

People change only when they choose to change, not when someone wants them to. I needed to worry about the larger group, not just the one difficult participant. I also learned to check my ego.

I've since met other participants with Zoon-like tendencies and, trust me, I learned from my mistake.

Building Your Action Plan: Difficult Participant Mistakes

My top three mistakes are:

1. _____

2. _____

3. _____

My action steps to correct these mistakes are:

1. _____

2. _____

3. _____

I'm committed to correcting these mistakes because:

_____

_____

_____

6

Co-Facilitation Mistakes

I've enjoyed rewarding experiences with many of the co-facilitators I've shared the platform with, and I've also worked with people who have added gray hairs to my mustache. If the two trainers don't connect, then running a session together can seem like walking through a minefield blindfolded. The more they try to stay out of each other's way, the more they continue their "tension convention." "Co-facilitator clash" is the name for it, and participants can quickly sense the lack of synergy. Their egregious behavior can lead to participant disinterest, favoritism, and lack of buy-in regarding the material that's being presented. Co-facilitators can sabotage each other in a variety of ways, for example, by leaving the room, reading the newspaper, or working on the computer in the back of the room while the other facilitator is presenting. Sometimes thoughtless co-facilitators repeatedly exceed their agreed-upon time limit. The result can be a ruined relationship, bitterness, and failure of the workshop.

The solidarity, trust, and connection between two co-facilitating trainers is vital to the session's outcome. So many factors can be affected if their working relationship evokes thoughts of feuding attorneys. Their teamwork must be real and flawless.

What can get in the way? Ego, insecurity, personal agendas, lack of commitment, lack of preparation, and dislike are typical contributors. Communication and a common goal are musts for the two trainers to flourish. To create more Ginger Rogers and Fred Astaire moments and fewer Ike and Tina Turner bouts in the classroom, explore the 10 co-facilitator mistakes discussed in this chapter. As you're reading the mistakes, consider some of the people you facilitate with and determine if any of these factors prevail. Then commit to Jim's Gems to cement your partnership. Think about this, too: Just because your co-facilitator hasn't had a heart-to-heart discussion with you about some of these mistakes doesn't mean they don't exist.

Mistake #1:
Leaving the room while your co-facilitator is presenting

Jim's Gems:

◆ To show commitment and camaraderie, stay in the room to support your co-facilitator unless there's an emergency to deal with.

To avoid workshop road rage with your co-facilitator, if you must leave the room, don't stay away for an extended period of time; don't keep running in and out of the room either. Check in with him or her upon your return.

◆ While you're in the room you can take notes of important points made, complete a co-facilitator evaluation sheet, and scan the room for raised hands your co-facilitator might have missed. You can also follow along with the program to be prepared to add your thoughts if called upon.
◆ Remain in the room to help deal with difficult participant behavior.

Mistake #2:
Making noise or distractions in the back of the room while your co-facilitator is presenting

Jim's Gems:

◆ Refrain from making noise in the back of the room. For instance, don't work on your flipchart or tear off flipchart pages;

don't use your cell phone or computer; don't read newspapers or other materials unrelated to the presentations; don't carry on side conversations with participants; don't sigh, groan, give frustrated looks, or try to facilitate from the back of the room.

Avoid facilitating the progress of a sign-in sheet while your co-facilitator is presenting. This is distracting.

◆ Do not walk around in the back of the room. Try to remain stationary or seated.

◆ Don't engage in side conversations with any managers in the back of the room while your co-facilitator is presenting. Such chat is niggling and disrespectful.

Mistake #3:
Not paying attention while your co-facilitator is presenting

Jim's Gems:

◆ To be the consummate partner, stay focused on the discussion and room dynamics.

◆ Avoid doing work or checking things off your to-do list.

◆ Avoid having to put a considerable amount of time into planning for your segment. After all, you already should be thoroughly prepared. An occasional glance or a brief review is fine, just to refresh your memory.

Be prepared to step in and add your views if your co-facilitator is in a jam.

Mistake #4:
Answering a question for your co-facilitator before you were given the OK signal

Jim's Gems:

◆ Do not think that just because you have had a similar experience you have the right to immediately share your perspective. Ask for permission and once it's given, share your experience second.

To avoid a major blowup with your co-facilitator, do not—let me repeat—do not answer for your co-facilitator unless you ask and receive permission to do so.

- ◆ Don't ever put words in your co-facilitator's mouth by saying, "What he meant to say was..." or "What I think she is trying to say is..."
- ◆ Talk to your co-facilitator during the break to discuss your views.
- ◆ When you do provide an answer, begin by saying something in this vein, "An additional way of thinking about this is..."
- ◆ Do not upstage or try to outdo your co-facilitator. Remember you're working as a team.

Mistake #5:
Going over your allotted facilitation time limit

Jim's Gems:
- ◆ Change your mindset from thinking that your co-facilitator is always going to be able to bail you out by shortening his or her part.
- ◆ Prepare for the time you were given.

Avoid going over your designated time, especially if you have corrected your co-facilitator for doing the same.

- ◆ When your co-facilitator has segued to your presentation, do not spend an additional amount of time covering information your co-facilitator has covered or is going to cover because you think he or she has not done a credible job or is not going to cover it as thoroughly as you think you might.
- ◆ Avoid these excuses, and the like, for running over: "We were really into the discussion. I didn't want to stop it." "That activity always goes great when you let it run its entire course." "If I had stopped it, they would not have gotten the point." "I just had to make that one final point."

Mistake #6:
Not developing signals for sharing

Jim's Gems:

◆ To enhance communication and teamwork, develop signals before the session that the two of you can use when either one of you wants to communicate something when you're not presenting. Signals can include standing up, waving your hand, or eyebrow arching.

◆ To make the signal most effective, determine how long you're going to signal before you stop.
For instance, if I'm the person presenting and I see your signal but choose not to take your comment after 30 to 60 seconds, that should signal to you that I've decided to move forward with the workshop. Avoid nonstop signaling.

Never come up to the front of the room talking or distributing handouts while your co-facilitator is presenting.

◆ Develop a bond of trust regarding the signals.

Mistake #7:
Disagreeing with your co-facilitator in front of the group

Jim's Gems:

◆ Disagree during breaks or before and after the session. Never disagree in front of the group.

◆ Use language that suggests you're working as a team. Offer additional viewpoints, not opposing viewpoints. If the point your co-facilitator is making is slightly off base, discuss it during an impromptu break and suggest that he or she correct the inaccuracy in front of the group. If you are facilitating and you feel unsure about a point you're trying to make, ask for help.

◆ If the point the person is making is absolutely incorrect, ask for permission to offer another viewpoint. You and your co-facilitator should have established an "absolutely wrong answer" signal in advance.

Mistake #8:
Lacking chemistry with your co-facilitator

Jim's Gems:

◆ Practice often to develop teamwork and synergy.

◆ Develop trust about providing and receiving feedback. Offer both positive and polishing feedback. Accept all feedback graciously and work to apply it.

◆ Develop smooth ways to transition or hand off to each other.

◆ Use each other's name when reminding the group of points each of you made during the workshop.

Learn the entire program so that you don't limit yourself to the parts you feel comfortable with. Share the responsibility for facilitating the various modules.

◆ Learn your co-facilitator's facilitation strengths, likes, and weaknesses.

◆ Constantly look for ways to support each other during the session.

◆ Discuss the workshop during breaks.

◆ Remind each other about what you each need. Let him or her know what type of support you need.

◆ Avoid eating off your co-facilitator's plate; that is, don't cover information he or she is going to cover and don't use his or her facilitation time.

◆ Spend time together outside of your office and the training classroom.

Mistake #9:
Bringing your personal agenda to the session

Jim's Gems:

◆ Leave your agenda at home. If your co-facilitator calls your attention to it, listen and respond to the feedback. Seek to understand before you seek to be understood.

Ask your co-facilitator to send you a signal if he or she senses that you are moving back into the personal agenda during your facilitation.

- ◆ Do some soul-searching. Ask yourself what's causing the agenda.
- ◆ Level with your co-facilitator early that you are struggling with some "me" issues regarding the content.
- ◆ Ask your co-facilitator for help in helping you move past or through your agenda.

Mistake #10:
Relying on your co-facilitator always to facilitate the parts you're uncomfortable with or don't like doing

Jim's Gems:

- ◆ Learn and understand what's needed to deliver all of the session's modules.
- ◆ Work with your co-facilitator to prepare for those parts, but do not facilitate the parts exactly the same way he or she does. Develop your own method and style for delivering them.

Stretch yourself by delivering content you're not familiar with.

- ◆ Continue to ask for feedback on how you're doing.
- ◆ Keep practicing to polish your skills. Don't just deliver the uncomfortable modules once or twice a year.
- ◆ Research the material that you find challenging and observe others facilitating it.

In the Trenches

Tony dreaded co-facilitating with Madhu. The two just didn't work well together. They had different beliefs, different styles, and different personalities. He was charismatic, high energy, and creative. She was meticulous, relentless, and omniscient (at least she came across that way). If you asked Tony what the problem was, he would ask you to take a seat and point-by-point share with you his mountain of concerns. If you asked Madhu, she would offer, "Problem? I didn't know we had a problem. Tony just needs to learn all the facets of the program and deliver it as it's designed to be delivered. He'll be fine."

Tony would have sleepless nights leading up to his workshops with Madhu. He would anguish over the energy he wasted just dreading the eight or 16 excruciating hours he'd have to spend with her co-facilitating the workshop. Each time he'd plan, prepare, and pray not to get upset or annoyed by anything she did. He said it was important that the participants not see any discord. He routinely talked about "taking one for the team" whenever the two were paired.

Their sessions usually began on a good note, but Madhu, in Tony's view, would quickly do something that would aggravate him. He even wondered, at times, if he was just waiting for her to make a mistake. Their workshop feedback sessions would end abruptly, too, with the two trainers disagreeing, like two political candidates during a heated debate, about how the session went and how they rated each other's performance.

Before this particular workshop, Madhu reminded Tony about how important timing was. They were delivering a new program to a new client, and they had to cover all of the material. Tony agreed and said he would do his best. He listened intently to her guidance, knowing that he did have a tendency to go longer than needed because of his very interactive style.

Madhu began the session, moving purposefully through the introductions, objectives, agenda, and opening comments. She then covered the next two modules, finishing the last module 20 minutes late. Smoldering in the back of the room, Tony waited for the handoff. "I can't believe she went over," he thought to himself, "especially after telling me that I need to pay attention to the clock." Madhu then turned the session over to Tony, and he took it from there. The participants could not see his dissatisfaction, but inwardly he was livid. As Tony was preparing to wrap up his segment he was approaching the time he needed to finish, according to the agenda. However, he believed he could take all of the allotted time to cover his module since Madhu had exceeded her time limit by 20 minutes. He thought that she would have to make up the time during her next segment.

Madhu had another plan in mind as she stood up, grabbed the handouts, and walked to the front of the room while Tony was in midsentence, saying, "Excuse me, Tony, thanks for covering that so nicely. I think it's a great time to distribute these handouts, and I'll take it from here." He considered not budging when she came up to the front, but he didn't want the participants to notice the friction. Instead, Tony walked to the back of the room to the trainer's table, smiling but seething on the inside, as Madhu was distributing the handouts. He waited for the lunch break to share his thoughts with Madhu. It wasn't pretty.

The two have not worked together since.

 Building Your Action Plan: Co-Facilitation Mistakes

My top three mistakes are:

1. _____

2. _____

3. _____

My action steps to correct these mistakes are:

1. _____

2. _____

3. _____

I'm committed to correcting these mistakes because:

_____

_____

_____

7

Storytelling Mistakes

A picture is worth a thousand words, but a well-told story might be worth two thousand. Storytelling is a vanishing art that takes years to perfect. Once you have it mastered, though, you're able to take your sessions, presentations, and workshops to unbelievable heights.

Why tell stories? How do they help learners retain information and audiences remember important points? For starters, storytelling can make vague concepts become concrete and help lectures and other dry material become easier to absorb and remember. Storytelling is a powerful and memorable way to open or close a session. It's also a clever way to enhance your credibility at the beginning of the session without sounding or appearing pompous and haughty. Storytelling also helps you engage your learner's head and heart. And, you can take storytelling to an even more amazing place if you add dramatic and theatrical touches while telling the story.

Stand-up comedians and spoken-word artists come to mind when I think of awesome storytellers. They truly give eyes to your ears. Excellent storytelling ability not only is a critical skill, but also it can propel you into the stratosphere of renowned facilitators, speakers, trainers, and presenters.

Not all who tell stories do it well, though. Many don't know the essential steps and nuances of powerful storytelling. This deficit leads to myriad mistakes. Although this chapter will not prepare you for performing on Broadway or responding to casting calls, it will examine 13 of the most prevalent storytelling mistakes made by presenters.

Mistake #1:
Telling your audience that you're about to tell a story

Jim's Gems:

◆ To avoid giving people an excuse not to listen, begin telling your story without letting your listeners know that it's coming.

Another way to start telling your story is by asking a question or by getting the audience involved. For example, you could ask, "By a show of hands, how many of you have...?"

◆ Begin telling your story by providing the setting.
◆ Make a critical learning point and then describe your story's setting and move into your story from there.

Mistake #2:
Concluding your story by informing the group what they should have learned from the story

Jim's Gems:

◆ Keep the participants engaged by asking them what they learned from the story.
◆ Ask the learners if they understood the point you were making by telling the story.
◆ After the group has responded to your answers, provide your learning point if it has not yet been shared.

Divide the group into discussion teams to talk about what they learned from your story.

◆ Stop the story three-quarters of the way through and ask the group to form teams to discuss how they think the story ends. Have them record and post their answers on flipcharts. Finish the story, and then review the answers they developed.

Mistake #3:
Not having a learning point or central lesson in your story

Jim's Gems:

♦ To avoid telling stories for the sake of telling stories, don't tell a story if it doesn't have a central learning point.

Avoid having too many lessons in one story.

♦ Develop the learning point first as you're preparing the story. Know your goal for the story or why you're telling that particular story.

♦ Make sure your story lesson is content related.

♦ Don't hide the lesson so deep within the story that people cannot determine what it is.

Mistake #4:
Not providing meaningful details and descriptions early in the story

Jim's Gems:

♦ To give your listeners a clear picture of the time and place of the story, develop the story setting early. Describe the time of year, scenery, characters, colors, weather, and so forth.

♦ Move slowly through your descriptions.

♦ Repeat some of the details if necessary to give the listeners a great sense of the setting.

♦ Use names of key players—your wife or husband, neighbor, manager, daughter, or others.

♦ Also, use powerful gestures and visuals to describe the setting, not just words.

Mistake #5:
Not putting your whole self into the story by using dramatic techniques

Jim's Gems:

♦ For a more memorable effect, act out the story as you're telling it. Use gestures, movement, and dialog.

*Choose audience members
to be dialog targets as
you're acting out
conversations.*

- Vary the tone and rate of your speech.
- To connect with your listeners, come into the group as you're telling the story and have fun with it (if appropriate).
- Put your heart and soul into the story.
- For dramatic effect, use pauses.
- To help with retention, use props.

Mistake #6:
Taking too long to tell the story

Jim's Gems:

- To avoid losing your listeners, limit your stories to approximately three to five minutes during your workshops. If you do tell a longer story, make sure your next one is shorter. For keynote speeches, you can lengthen your story. Awesome keynote speakers' stories range anywhere from 10 to 15 minutes or longer.
- If you're not sure how long your stories last, use a timer or ask your co-facilitator to signal to you when you've gone beyond your intended time goal.
- To avoid turning people off, don't be preachy.

*To trim the fat from your
story, avoid redundancy
and eliminate
unnecessary details
and facts.*

- Look for cues, such as frustrated, disinterested looks or yawns, from your audience to determine if it's time to wrap up.
- Remember that the most important people in the room are your audience members. Don't put them to sleep with a long, drawn-out story about how you saved the world with one arm tied behind your back, blindfolded, in the dead of winter, during a hailstorm, without any boots or gloves, while hopping on one foot, carrying 250 pounds of equipment, and without having any food for two months.
- Practice telling your story first in front of a mirror or video-camera, then for your family, friends, or colleagues. Ask for feedback about what works, what doesn't, what was unclear, and what should be cut.

Mistake #7:
Making insensitive comments during the story

Jim's Gems:

◆ Don't use profanity during your story.

◆ Know your organization's culture. Avoid making comments that would offend someone by poking fun at people's age, sexual orientation, gender, race, physical ability, ethnicity, educational level, socioeconomic class, speech, and so forth.

◆ To avoid offending someone, don't mention another organization's name during your story unless it's a positive story and you're giving the company kudos.

◆ Know your audience and what's going on in the company (for example, downsizing, a merger or acquisition, a death, a firing).

Mistake #8:
Not giving credit where credit is due

Jim's Gems:

◆ Take advantage of the great stories that have been told in history and literature. Use or adapt them to suit your presentation needs. Just be sure to give proper attribution to the original writer or speaker of the words.

◆ Do not memorize others' words; rather, adhere to the story line and quote memorable phrases, but use your own words and mannerisms to make the story come naturally to you.

Be sure the story is relevant to the objectives of the presentation. Otherwise, your learners will be scratching their heads trying to figure out the connection.

◆ Trim the story to meet your time limitations.

◆ Choose stories that are relatively unknown so that they will be fresh for your audience. Nobody wants to hear *The Little Engine That Could*[1] again!

---

[1]Piper, W. (1959). *The Little Engine That Could.* New York: Plat & Munk Company.

Mistake #9:
Failing to end your story with a call to action

Jim's Gems:

♦ For better story transfer, sound a call to action—a challenge to your listeners to embark on a task or take some action—at the end of your story.

♦ Encourage them to do something that they've never attempted before.

♦ Move into the group and have them repeat after you the call to action.

Have them turn to the person sitting closest to them and tell them what they're going to do differently because of your story.

♦ Focus on several audience members for three to five seconds each, maintaining a single thought for each person as you issue your call to action.

♦ To avoid coming off aggressively, don't point at your audience members when you're providing your call to action.

♦ Use appropriate language for the call to action: "I challenge you to..." "I encourage you to..." or "If you're ever in a situation like this, remember to..." Avoid saying, "I need you to..." "I'm telling you to..." or "You have to..."

Mistake #10:
Failing to take your audience on an emotional roller coaster during the story

Jim's Gems:

♦ Change the volume of your voice to take people up and down during your story.

♦ Use powerful, dramatic gestures to create an emotional roller coaster.

Use pauses to build emotion and suspense.

♦ Repeat important phrases to generate emotion.

♦ Use movement to tug at emotion.

♦ Don't cry alligator tears, but if you find yourself becoming emotional, don't try to hold it in. Keep it real.

Mistake #11:
Telling the story too fast

Jim's Gems:

- Avoid rushing through your story. You don't want to lose your listeners.
- So your meanings and points are not lost, enunciate all your words and avoid clipping your endings by saying such things as "gonna" instead of "going to."
- Have a solid beginning, middle, and conclusion for your story.

Use dialog during your story. Don't just tell the group what someone said; instead, become the person and show the group how that person talks.

- Consider the timing before you tell your story. If time is too short, don't try to squeeze your story in by rushing.
- Get audience members involved as you relate a story.

Mistake #12:
Bending the story too much

Jim's Gems:

- A little theater and drama are fine, but don't introduce too much sensationalism in your story. You will lose your audience and they will question the story's authenticity.
- Be consistent when citing dates, statistics, and times during your story.
- Avoid creating too many emotional ups and downs during the story.
- Make the point without breaking the point by belaboring it.
- Be careful not to use your story to fulfill a personal agenda.

Avoid being the hero in all of your stories. It's OK to be the zero—the person who made a mistake—and then you can share what you learned from that experience. Consider this: When you're telling a gory story, use yourself as the main character, and when you're telling a glory story, use someone else as the main character.

Mistake #13:
Failing to build a connection with your listeners

Jim's Gems:

◆ At the beginning and at the end of your story, use words and phrases that build connections with your listeners: "How many of you have had a similar experience?" "I trust that many of you have been in a similar jam." "I know that people in your profession are faced with challenges like this every day." "We've all worked for bad bosses at one time in our lives, haven't we?"

Don't just tell the story, be the story.

When you build the connection at the end, your call to action should immediately follow.

◆ Use eye contact and inviting gestures to build connections with your group.

◆ Be real and have fun.

In the Trenches

Most speaker introductions are short and sweet and that's what I expected from Trang. He asked if he could introduce me before my next workshop and I obliged. My one and only request was that he make it brief.

I was working with my client facilitating two 2-day workshops in a week. Trang's group was first; the workshop was scheduled for Monday and Tuesday. I would repeat the same session for another group of trainers on Wednesday and Thursday. The back-to-back workshops didn't bother me at all. I love working with trainers, and this was a fantastic organization.

Trang mentioned that the main reason he wanted to introduce me was that he was really thrilled about the workshop. He had been with the organization for several years and was considered one its elite trainers. "Very seldom do I give compliments, Jim, but your workshop was just what I needed," he said. "I thought I was a pretty good trainer, but you showed some new things that I could use right away. I want to introduce you and let the other people know what they're in for." That sounded fair enough. A personal endorsement and testimonial from a current staff member usually goes over quite well.

As planned, Trang showed up on Wednesday morning right on time. We spoke briefly while I was setting up. Still buzzing from the session he had just attended, Trang shared how pumped he was to be doing the introduction. I thanked him again and reminded him that the shorter the introduction, the better. "No problem, Jim, I'll take care of it," he said. When it was time for the workshop to begin, I took my seat in the back of the room and waited for Trang to introduce me to the group. Feeling pretty charged myself, I was ready for another high-energy two days.

Trang began the introduction by highlighting how much he learned during his two-day session. At that point, I thought he was going to bring the introduction to a close, so I stood up and started to slowly walk to the front of the room. But, he continued. He began to tell a story about how before he became a trainer he used to be in sales. "Where is he going?" I thought to myself. "What does book sales have to do with me facilitating a train-the-trainer workshop?" Becoming confused and bothered, I motioned to Trang to cut it short. It was too late; he went from trainer to Leno right before my very eyes.

His story went pretty much like this: Before becoming a corporate trainer, he used to sell books with three other fellows. The four men would ride around town each day, selling their books and magazines. What used to bother Trang and two of the other guys was that their colleague, Barry, was outselling all of them. What made this hard to stomach was that Barry stuttered. One day, the guys pulled into a fast-food restaurant to get lunch. Before they got out of the car, they con-fronted Barry and asked him for his secret. They wanted to know how he was able to sell so many books while they were batting zero.

Pretending to stutter like Barry, Trang continued with the story. "The, the reason, I, I, I guess, pe-people wa-wa-want to ba-buy from, from me is because they wa-wa-would rather ba-buy the bo-bo-book than hear me ma-ma-make my sales pitch."

Trang finished, "Don't worry, you will not have any difficulties understanding Jim's message. He's a phenomenal trainer! With that, I bring you Jim Smith Jr."

I was stunned! You could have driven an 18-wheeler into my mouth as I stood in the corner with my mouth open. I walked to the front of the room, shook Trang's hand, and waited for him to leave. I immediately introduced myself and gave the group a quick assignment. I told them to take 30 seconds in their small groups and discuss what they liked or disliked about Trang's opening story. I sensed that every single person had been offended by the story, but I wanted them to share and compare their views. When I brought the groups together, what I anticipated was sadly true. They hated the story! Moreover, they couldn't understand what it had to do with the workshop.

I piggybacked on their frustrations and encouraged them never to tell stories or tell jokes that offended others. It proved to be a very poignant moment. I thought to myself, "Thanks, I guess, Trang, for the opening and for being my case study." I next moved into my opening introductory activity. Each person had to create a business card for their partner, highlighting something about their partner's past, future, and workshop expectations. I then asked them to stand and introduce their partner to the large group. Four introductions later, Kristin stood to introduce her partner. As she began her introduction, she started to tear up. "Well, in my partner's past," she began, "she used to stutter. Hearing that awful story reminded her how mean people can be." The room went cemetery quiet.

Building Your Action Plan: Storytelling Mistakes

My top three mistakes are:

1. _____

2. _____

3. _____

My action steps to correct these mistakes are:

1. _____
2. _____
3. _____

I'm committed to correcting these mistakes because:

_____
_____
_____

8

Evaluation Mistakes

Evaluations mean so much but often are given so little consideration. Time and time again, trainers bemoan the fact that their evaluations are seldom completed although they never pause to consider their own role in the process. In more than 20 years of training and speaking, I've observed the same evaluation practice wherever I've gone. Trainers wait to the final seconds of the class to distribute the evaluation and then expect their learners to complete them thoroughly.

The evaluation's length and design also determine how comprehensively learners complete them. Participants are typically in a rush to get out of the room. In many cases, the only thing standing between them and their freedom is their circling the ratings that best reflect their workshop thoughts and feelings. Then, they sprint out of the room leaving the comment lines blank unless they've had an unusually compelling or morbid experience.

To give your evaluations more importance and meaning, consider the information shared in this chapter. The mistakes that are discussed occur as often as many of the ones mentioned in previous chapters. It's ironic that evaluations are supposed to measure the workshop's effectiveness, thereby, in some regard, determining the trainer's value to the organization, but they're treated like items that are left on layaway by a Christmas shopper who has run out of money. Look at this top-ten list of evaluation mistakes, and then develop an action plan for what you're going to do differently. You'll be pleased with the results.

Mistake #1:
Waiting until the last five minutes of the session to distribute the evaluations

Jim's Gems:

◆ To ensure that your evaluations are completed more comprehensively, distribute the evaluations at the beginning, halfway point, or three-quarter mark of the session.

*Remind learners to use their break time
to begin completing their evaluations.*

◆ Have participants work in pairs or trios to complete the evaluation together.
◆ Give participants time to complete the evaluation after each module.

Mistake #2:
Failing to design the evaluation to elicit more participant feedback and comments

Jim's Gems:

◆ Provide space for comments under each module or objective question on the evaluation.
◆ Make sure to write, "Please turn over" at the bottom right-hand corner of the evaluation if you want your participants to answer the questions on the back.
◆ Alternate a rating question with a comment question throughout your evaluation.

Put space for narrative comments and remarks near the top (the first half) of the evaluation. People tend to have more "evaluation writing energy" when they start completing the form than when they are finishing it.

Mistake #3:
Failing to introduce the evaluation by highlighting its significance

Jim's Gems:

◆ Before distributing evaluation forms, highlight the value of the evaluation process. Discuss how comprehensive participant evaluation feedback helps the organization, the program, and the facilitator.

◆ Avoid belittling comments aimed at evaluation completion: "Here's the part of the day everyone dreads. That's right, completing the evaluation." "I know you've already found it in the workbook, so just take a minute or two fill it out." "Here's that thing that they say we have to get you to complete." "The only thing that stands between you and the door is the completion of the evaluation." Instead, try: "I want to thank you for a fantastic day. To take this workshop to an even higher level, we'd like you to consider today's experience and capture your thoughts on our evaluation," or "I'm introducing this wonderful feedback tool to you early. Please give us your candid feedback so that we can continue to improve our program," or "Your comments and ratings will go a long way in helping us provide the results-based training we all want."

◆ After collecting the evaluations, carefully review them and note any immediate changes you have to make, place them in a folder or envelope so that they're not destroyed, and put them in a safe place until you're able to file them with the other workshop evaluations. Develop a measurement system so that you can develop reports that review the workshop's effectiveness.

Mistake #4:
Failing to provide space on the evaluation for participants to evaluate more than just the workshop, the materials, and the facilitator

Jim's Gem:

◆ In addition to providing space for participants to evaluate the facilitator and the workshop, provide space on the evaluation for the learners to evaluate their participation, the A/V and visual aids, the other participants, and how successful they think they're going to be when incorporating their new knowledge, skills, or abilities back on the job.

Mistake #5:
Failing to provide space on the evaluation for participants to highlight how they're going to apply what they have learned

Jim's Gems:

◆ When developing your evaluation, highlight questions that will get participants to think about how to use their new learning back on the job. Include questions such as these: "How do you plan to incorporate today's learning back on the job?" "What challenges do you anticipate?" "Where can we reach you in 30 (or 60) days to follow up to see how you're using your new skills?" "Moving forward, how would you like for us to support you?"

◆ Include questions on your evaluation form to help learners consider how they are going to gain their managers' support: "How are you going to work with your manager to sustain your energy and momentum?" "What additional ongoing support do you think you're going to need?"

Mistake #6:
Failing to provide space on the evaluation for participants to highlight their learning goals

Jim's Gems:

◆ To develop more individual ownership, buy-in, and accountability, provide space at the top of the evaluation for participants to list their top two to three learning goals.

◆ To foster networking and socialization, have participants share their learning goals with a learning partner.

◆ To create more accountability and responsibility, have them exchange one learning goal with their learning partner (at the beginning of the session) that they'd like their learning partner to be responsible for during the workshop.

Mistake #7:
Failing to provide space on the evaluation for participants to highlight how their organization will benefit from their training

Jim's Gem:

◆ Near the end of the evaluation, provide space for participants to list three ways their organization or department could benefit from their training experience.

Mistake #8:
Using an evaluation that is mostly a ratings critique ("smile sheet")

Jim's Gem:

◆ Develop your evaluation so that it allows space for positive or constructive comments, ratings, application statements, and action plan steps.

Mistake #9:
Failing to thank participants for helping with your evaluation effort

Jim's Gem:

◆ From a customer service and thoughtfulness perspective, write a "Thank you for completing this evaluation" greeting somewhere near the top or bottom of the form.

Mistake #10:
Making noise or creating distractions as the participants are completing their evaluations

Jim's Gem:

◆ To limit distractions and other noise that disturb learners while they are completing the evaluation, avoid talking to them, taking flipchart paper off the walls, ripping and throwing away paper, cleaning the tables, or leaving and entering the room.

In the Trenches

Jasmine and Sergei put the finishing touches on another powerful diversity session. The two trainers were confident that the learners were walking away with plenty to consider and plenty to apply. Many students stayed after the session to continue the dialog. Several were there to show their appreciation; the others were searching for additional tips for dealing with their diversity dilemmas.

While Jasmine was wrapping up her final conversations, Sergei went around to each table to collect the evaluations. Reading and collecting at the same time, he was making little progress. Jasmine eventually joined him and the two collected all of the evaluations. Following their post-session ritual, they met at the back table to discuss them.

Thirty minutes and 25 evaluations later, the two trainers, though exhausted, were grinning from ear to ear. Twenty-three of the evaluations rated the session as "excellent" and the other two as "very good." The comments were also extremely positive. They hugged, high-fived, then briefly discussed the next day's session. This was day one of three consecutive one-day sessions, and they had gotten off to a laudable start. Sergei said that he would clean up the room and meet Jasmine for a celebratory drink in about a half hour. Fortunately for them, the training was being held at a golf resort, and the bar was only 20 steps away. Jasmine left as Sergei readied the room for the next day.

When Jasmine arrived in the morning for the second day of training, Sergei was already in the room standing at the back trainer's table looking as though he had just seen a ghost. "Sergei, what's wrong with you?" she asked. "Jas, Jas, I can't find the evaluations! I've looked everywhere! Have you seen them?" "No, you cleaned up yesterday," she said. "Where did you put them last?" "Over there, with the other extra supplies," he said, pointing to an empty table in the front corner of the room. "I marked them with yesterday's date, put them in a folder, and left them with the other extras."

As he was finishing his statement, one of the resort's banquet managers came in to see if the room was setup appropriately for the training. They both commented that the room was fine but that they couldn't find the evaluations. The manager asked where they had last seen them. "Over there," Sergei said, pointing to the table he had pointed to when Jasmine asked him the same question. The manager's look turned to alarm. "What's wrong?" Sergei asked, "You look worried." "Our cleaning staff comes in every night, and they're instructed to clean and clear off every table and throw the trash away," she said. "We didn't have any trash on that table; we just put our extra supplies there," Sergei said. "And now that I think about it, the other supplies are gone too! Are you telling me that the cleaning crew trashed all of our stuff?" "I believe so," she said.

"I can't believe it," Sergei continued. "One of the best sessions I've ever facilitated and I don't have any evaluations to show for it. I can't believe it! This stinks. Bruce [their manager] is going to go berserk. From now on, I'm going to keep all my evaluations with me until I get back to the office. They're too valuable to leave just lying around. Darn!"

Building Your Action Plan: Evaluation Mistakes

My top three mistakes are:

1. _____

2. _____

3. _____

My action steps to correct these mistakes are:

1. _____

2. _____

3. _____

I'm committed to correcting these mistakes because:

_____

_____

_____

9

Presentation Mistakes

Perhaps the number one component of a successful workshop is powerful and polished presentation skills. The ability to communicate and engage people with your eyes, gestures, movement, stories, humor, information, and pace is so critical. Some speakers make it look effortless and poetic, but others make you want to shout, sleep, or sneak out of the room. Nevertheless, to remain effective in the classroom, facilitators—whether novice or tenured—need to continue to hone their presentation skills.

From poorly handling questions to using too many acronyms, the mistakes are countless. Twenty-two of the top mistakes are reviewed in this chapter, but this chapter could probably include 1,000 more. Careful consideration should be given to this chapter because there's more to making a successful presentation than just standing up and disseminating information. I become embarrassed and annoyed at conferences and seminars when I see cream-of-the-crop professionals in my industry essentially sleepwalk through their presentations with little animation, movement, creativity, or flair. I want to shout to the participants, "Don't clap, don't clap! You've paid too much money to be here. Tell them to polish their presentation and facilitation skills."

As an industry, we need to get better. As managers, leaders, sales professionals, and teachers, we could certainly step up in this area too. Remember, the sterling presentation is more than just words and visuals. You have to connect with your audience. You have to know your audience. You have to move your audience—cognitively and affectively. Two of my favorite quotes are, "Just because it was said doesn't mean it made it to my head" and "Just because you taught it doesn't mean I bought it or caught it." Great presenters have very few holes in their presentation-skills net.

Mistake #1:
Failing to use eye communication

Jim's Gems:

◆ To help connect with your audience while presenting, focus on the eyes of your listeners. If that poses a problem, focus on the nose or forehead of the listeners.

Use your eyes to engage people. At some point, each person in your session should feel as though he or she experienced a personal connection with you.

◆ Maintain eye contact with each person for at least three to six seconds.
◆ When maintaining eye contact, use the STOP (single thought, one person) method.
◆ Use your eyes to emphasize key points.

Mistake #2:
Relying excessively on acronyms, abbreviations, and jargon

Jim's Gems:

◆ When presenting, avoid acronyms, slang, and jargon. Speak clearly. Communicate confidently, warmly, and with purpose. Remember that language is powerful. You don't want to lose or confuse your listeners.

Use words that clearly communicate the content, meaning, and feeling of your message.

Mistake #3:
Avoiding movement and gestures

Jim's Gems:

- Make sure your movement is purposeful. Do not wander aimlessly around the room.
- To help with your movement, visit your workshop or meeting room beforehand for familiarity.
- When presenting at the front of the room, move in an arc to get to both sides of the room.
- Use movement when telling stories to add theater and passion and to emphasize key points.

To avoid appearing stiff, formal, or professorial, avoid the lectern.

- Move into your listeners. Present from various spots in the room. When you move to a new location, stay there for at least 30 to 60 seconds.
- Make your gestures natural; don't under- or overuse them.
- Remember that gestures communicate your energy, spirit, and enthusiasm.
- Do not keep your hands in your pockets.
- To help with participant retention and emphasis, use the fingers of one hand to indicate totals that are five or less.
- Know and avoid your nervous tendencies and habits.

Mistake #4:
Not using vocal variety or voice inflection

Jim's Gems:

- Use animation and vocal variety when speaking to avoid droning on in a monotone voice.
- Be sure to breathe while speaking; breathing relaxes your voice.
- Sound, appear, and be interested in your topic.
- Focus on your pace, pausing, resonance, and intonation.

Be mindful not to let your voice trail off at the end of your sentences.

- Use voice inflection to emphasize key points, especially when telling stories or covering dry material.
- Lower your voice for dramatic effects.

Mistake #5:
Appearing closed

Jim's Gems:

- Smile often when presenting.
- Use open gestures.
- Move among your listeners.
- Use your participants' names.
- Provide personal experiences, especially those where you learned a valuable lesson through your mistake. Give your learners an opportunity to get to know you.
- Talk to your participants before the session or presentation, during the break, and at the session's end.

Mistake #6:
Using too many filler words (ah, OK, uh, um, so, you know)

Jim's Gems:

- When finishing a thought, pause before moving to your next point.
- Ask a colleague to observe you and provide feedback to help identify when you are likely to use filler words and what filler words you use.
- Record yourself to see where you can make improvements.
- Listen to your voicemail greeting to hear how others hear you.
- Don't get too comfortable and relaxed when presenting. Remember you're always on. To that end, consider what you're about to say, then speak slowly and clearly.

Mistake #7:
Talking to the screen

Jim's Gems:

- When presenting, avoid staring at and talking to the screen. Maintain eye contact with your audience as much as possible.

- Don't read directly from the screen or ask your audience members to do so. Paraphrase and ask the participants to paraphrase the information that's on the screen.
- If you have to read directly from the screen, walk to the side or stand behind your listeners. Present from that part of the room until you're ready to move on without having to rely on the PowerPoint presentation.

Mistake #8:
Standing and staying behind the podium

Jim's Gems:

- Move among your audience.
- Use the podium just to check your notes. Once you've checked your notes, move away from the podium and continue presenting.
- Don't clutch or hold onto the podium.
- Use the podium for effect when you're trying to project a more studious look when making an important point.

Mistake #9:
Telling jokes

Jim's Gems:

- Avoid telling jokes; natural humor is best.
- Make light of normal, everyday occurrences and current events.
- Really tune in and listen to your audience. Be spontaneous, knowledgeable, and witty. Piggyback onto their comments.
- Poke fun at yourself.
- Add humor to your stories.

Mistake #10:
Trying to present like someone else

Jim's Gems:

- Develop your own style and know what that style is; know your niche.
- Avoid watching or listening to the same speaker or presenter over and over again. You will invariably mimic that person's tendencies and style. Observe a variety of presenters.

- Get feedback from others on your style.
- Develop a style you are comfortable with, and be true to yourself.
- If you're a conservative, laid-back presenter, create opportunities for your audience to provide the energy. Also, use your voice and plenty of movement.

Mistake #11:
Not articulating your words clearly

Jim's Gems:
- Carefully enunciate words and avoid clipping your endings.
- Yawn and stretch your mouth before you begin.
- Practice pronouncing words that give you trouble.
- Get feedback from others on words that you don't clearly articulate.

Mistake #12:
Failing to involve your group in your presentation

Jim's Gems:
- Use a variety of methods to involve your audience in your presentations. For example you can ask for a show of hands or ask them to talk briefly to the person sitting to their right or left.
- Ask the learners to repeat a quotation, phrase, statement, or learning point that you've said.
- Split the room in half and give each side a particular assignment.
- Encourage them to complete a statement you're about to make.
  - Ask them a question.
  - Have them practice a task with the person sitting to their right or left.
  - Have them stand to indicate if they think the correct answer to your question is true or false.
  - Go into the group when you're telling a story or making a point and use certain audience members as visual aids or dialog targets.

Have them provide certain sound effects (rain, water, wind, or cheering, for example) to assist with your storytelling.

Mistake #13:
Presenting to impress, not express

Jim's Gems:

- ◆ Don't try to impress your listeners with your vocabulary or experiences. Present candidly, assuredly, and humbly.
- ◆ Share experiences when you were the one who made a mistake.
- ◆ Use teambuilding pronouns (we and us); be mindful of the number of times you say "I."
- ◆ Admit it when you don't know something. Offer to get back to the questioner as soon as you uncover the answer.
- ◆ Don't drop names.
- ◆ Don't exaggerate your points or stories.
- ◆ Don't lie.
- ◆ Be real; don't be overly bubbly or too gregarious.
- ◆ Gradually share your credentials; don't unload them on your listeners.

Mistake #14:
Failing to establish credibility or presence early

Jim's Gems:

- ◆ Begin your presentation on a high note. Jump on your group early with plenty of energy, enthusiasm, and passion.
- ◆ Have your opener well prepared.
- ◆ Use connecting phrases that suggest you have something in common with your audience members.

Share your credibility or claim to fame through a story.

- ◆ If giving a keynote address, make sure during your opening to thank the people within the organization who made it possible for you to be there.
- ◆ Through your mannerisms, gestures, word choice, and confidence, give clear evidence that you have a special message for them.
- ◆ Do not open by speaking from behind the podium or lectern.

Mistake #15:
Handling questions improperly

Jim's Gems:

- Repeat the person's question before answering.
- At times, pose the question to the group before answering.
- Listen for the questioner's content, meaning, and feeling.
- Ask for clarification if necessary.
- Avoid showing negative feelings or going off on a tangent.
- Don't divert the question.
- Don't interrupt; let the questioner ask the question completely.
- Make transitions with your answers whenever possible.
- Move toward the questioner.

Begin answering the question by looking at the questioner. Then answer the question looking at all audience members. Finish answering the question by looking at the questioner.

Mistake #16:
Not incorporating enough diversity into your presentation

Jim's Gems:

- Use diversity in your visuals. Pictures and graphics should represent people of various races, ethnicities, and abilities.
- When offering examples, provide a mix of gender, age, race, physical ability, education, employee status, socioeconomic class, and so forth. Avoid stereotypes. For example, nurses could be male or female. Use names that represent a variety of nationalities.
- Use multiple forms of media.
- Use activities and lecture.

Mistake #17:
Rushing your close

Jim's Gems:

- Methodically move toward your close; then, clearly and purposefully conclude your presentation.

◆ Don't facilitate a question-and-answer (Q&A) session as your final closing. Do your final Q&A early enough to finish the presentation with your concluding thoughts and a call to action. You never want to finish a presentation with an unanswered question or a dry, rushed close.

Offer a close that leaves your listeners inspired, confident, and ready to apply the knowledge and skills you have equipped them with.

◆ Present your closer like your opener. It should be powerful, motivational, content related, and action oriented.

◆ Remember that your close is the last part of your presentation that your audience will see. It's possibly the aspect they will remember the most.

Mistake #18:
Not knowing your audience and failing to tap into their WIIFM ("What's in it for me?")

Jim's Gems:

◆ Collect as much information as you can about your audience before the session. You can do this through surveys, interviews, questionnaires, meetings, and organizational data.

◆ Use the information you collect when developing your presentation (for example, key learning points, metaphors, and stories).

◆ To connect with your audience, use their language when presenting.

◆ Use the information you collect to highlight the needs, challenges, and opportunities for your group.

Mistake #19:
Being preachy

Jim's Gems:

◆ Don't get up on your soapbox. Leave the personal agenda at home.

◆ Get your audience members involved to avoid being preachy.

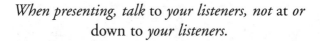

> *When presenting, talk to your listeners, not at or*
> down to *your listeners.*

◆ Create pictures with words. Give eyes to your listeners' ears so they can see what you're saying. Provide a vision for your listeners. Don't create a situation in which you frustrate your audience with a very one-sided and opinionated approach.

Mistake #20:
Using profanity

Jim's Gems:

◆ Under no circumstances should you use profanity! Don't even allude to a profane word.
◆ Be wary of using other offensive words or words that are related to profane words.
◆ Do not engage in "potty talk" by using words associated with bodily functions.

Mistake #21:
Apologizing for yourself or the organization

Jim's Gems:

◆ Stay away from situations where you find yourself saying you're sorry for something you or your organization did. For example, don't apologize for material you didn't cover.
◆ To avoid losing your credibility, do not begin your presentation by informing your audience that this is your first time covering the material.

Mistake #22:
Drawing on too many sports analogies or references

Jim's Gems:

◆ To connect with your audience, vary your examples when providing references, analogies, illustrations, and metaphors.

◆ Have examples that reflect all aspects of life, not just sports. Certainly Tiger Woods, Lance Armstrong, and Michael Jordan have contributed tremendously to our society, but there are other ways of highlighting teambuilding, personal power, resiliency, and confidence.

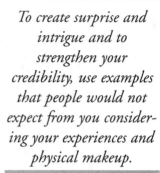

To create surprise and intrigue and to strengthen your credibility, use examples that people would not expect from you considering your experiences and physical makeup.

◆ To highlight your creativity and cleverness, use analogies that people haven't heard before.

◆ To develop more analogies and references, become more aware and observant as you move through life. Pay more attention to your experiences related to travel, work, family and parenting, customer service and shopping, cooking, learning, and television and movies.

In the Trenches

April recently attended a large human resources conference. Her management team sends the affable professional to the conference annually, and she looks forward to it throughout the year much as professionals anticipate their paychecks. She loves to learn from and share ideas with her colleagues and typically leaves the conference with enough renewed enthusiasm and energy to carry her through to the next year. April had every expectation that this year would be no different, looking forward to a high-impact, high-quality learning experience.

Sadly, the experience fell far short of her expectations. By the end of the first day of the conference, April had walked out of eight sessions. Eight sessions! Generally participants give the facilitators approximately 15 to 30 minutes to engage and connect with them, and April said that she painstakingly followed that protocol for the most part. Yet, by lunchtime on the next day, she had walked out of no fewer than 14 sessions. That afternoon, she was so disheartened she skipped the scheduled sessions and focused her efforts on informal learning and networking.

What specifically led to April's revolving-door workshop experiences? She told me in the span of two days, she had witnessed innumerable presentation and facilitation mistakes, enough to alienate her as a learner. She sat me down and began to vent:

♦ *Disaster Number One (Keep Your Eyes on the Prize—If You Can See It):* Imagine a large ballroom set up lecture style with seating for 400 people. Imagine 250 people in those seats, eager to hear what the presenters have to share. Now, imagine two presenters standing at the front of the room illustrating their main points on one tiny flipchart. What a disaster! Fewer than a dozen people in the room could actually see what the presenters were writing. To add insult to injury, the presenters kept saying such things as, "If you could see this, you'd really understand the point I'm trying to make." Most conference participants left the session less than 15 minutes into it.

♦ *Disaster Number Two (Hide and Go Speak):* A session on accelerated learning techniques featured a static PowerPoint presentation with the speaker in a far corner, in the dark, locked behind his podium, speaking in a monotone voice. Talk about conflicting subject matter and presentation style!

♦ *Disaster Number Three (Silence Is Golden—Not This Time):* In a session on creative training techniques, the speaker distributed a six-page, single-spaced handout and instructed the participants to read through the information quietly to themselves. The first 20 minutes of this session was spent in total silence—in a presentation on creative training techniques!

♦ *Disaster Number Four (We Are Family, but Not During My Session):* April and a colleague were sitting in the front row waiting for a session to begin. They were talking, laughing, and engaging in conversation with those around them. The presenter approached them and told them that their behavior would certainly not be acceptable once the session got started and if they didn't think they could control themselves they should just leave now. They accepted her invitation to leave.

April said she was flabbergasted by some of the other very basic presentation mistakes that ruined the conference for her. She indicated that she wasn't sure her management team would send her next year or if she even wanted to return.

Building Your Action Plan: Presentation Mistakes

My top three mistakes are:

1. _____

2. _____

3. _____

My action steps to correct these mistakes are:

1. _____

2. _____

3. _____

I'm committed to correcting these mistakes because:

_____

_____

_____

10

Get Out of
Your Own Way

Many of the methods for countering the mistakes mentioned in the previous chapters are common thoughts but not common practices. As I travel around the world, nationally and internationally, observing and coaching trainers, facilitators, managers, and speakers, I continue to see many of these same mistakes. Are these mistakes made in large part due to naïveté? Are they made because we don't receive timely and candid feedback? Are they made because we choose not to change, preferring to continue with our current speaking or training approach and style? Are they made because we don't think the mistakes are that critical to the presentations' overall outcome? Or, do we make the mistakes because we are apprehensive about stretching and trying something different? The answer is probably all of the above.

Something contributed to your decision to read this book, and I'm glad you did. Whether you've seen others make the mistakes or you make them yourself, you now know they exist, you know what they are, and you know that they influence the way listeners receive and retain the material. It's time to get out of your own way, stop making excuses, polish your skills, and amplify your personal power.

It's time to transform.

If you truly desire to be an outstanding presenter or trainer, someone who is coveted by organizations around the world, conferences, schools, professional groups, or by employees within your current organization, you should immediately begin to develop and implement your action plan (see the appendix). How? Begin working on the mistakes you recorded at the end of every chapter. Pull together your action plan by using the matrix provided in the appendix to this book.

Next, get footage of your presentations and make sure the camera pans the audience so that you can see the reactions. Tape record yourself and listen to how others hear you. You may also need to make a slight mindset adjustment to accept the notion that little mistakes mean a great deal to the overall effectiveness of any presentation or workshop. You'll get there!

Next, seek professional coaching, training, and feedback. Give yourself permission to get better.

Another transforming step is for you to make the decision to break through to truly awesome results. You have to let go of old habits. Rid yourself of presenter insecurity, ego, arrogance, denial, and fear. Let go of the "I've always done it this way" thinking. Your results will be immediate and rewarding.

There's so much more to presenting, training, and facilitating than just sharing information. I've seen powerful and timely information fall on deaf ears. I've seen many well-regarded and extremely bright leaders and subject matter experts soil their reputations by souring their listeners as they make monotone, mundane, lifeless, mistake-riddled presentations. Today's participants disengage quickly and they spread the news if you're not engaging.

I didn't attend college to be a trainer or speaker. Actually, I wanted to play professional football, write for *Sports Illustrated,* move into sports reporting, and then teach English at my former high school. I stumbled into what I'm doing now, but I couldn't have fallen into a better field. Whatever I did however, I would have been the same way—a stickler for details, doing things the right way and in an outstanding way.

I want your difference to make a difference. I want you to be special. I want you to blow people away. I want you to inspire, change, and motivate others. I want you to change behavior. I want the bathroom banter about you to be extremely positive. I want people to look forward to hearing you present or seeing you train. I want people to sprint to your meetings. I want you to get standing ovations because participants believe that you truly care about them and you don't merely see them as a warm body in a chair. I want you to commit to eliminating mistakes. I want the people who attend your sessions to want to come back for more.

What do you want?

Appendix

Crash and Learn: Your Complete Action Plan

Sustainability is the key to any wholesale change you make. Having an action plan holds you accountable for making necessary changes and ensuring that the changes are long lasting and meaningful.

Each chapter of *Crash and Learn* concluded with a brief exercise to serve as one component of your action plan for identifying and correcting mistakes in your presentations. This appendix presents a matrix to pull everything together and serve as your blueprint to mistake-free presenting. Take your time when completing the action plan. Ask others for their feedback and input. If necessary, get additional sheets of paper.

I wish you much success. Remember, the most important people in the room are your audience members. Treat them well. Inspire them. Create powerful behavioral change results for them. Help them tap into their potential.

Crash and Learn: My Complete Action Plan for Correcting Facilitation, Training, and Presentation Mistakes

Mistake Category (Chapter in *Crash and Learn*)	My Top Three Mistakes Are:	My Action Steps Include:	I'm Committed to Correcting These Mistakes Because:
Facilitation Mistakes (Chapter 1)	1. 2. 3.	1. 2. 3.	
Room Setup Mistakes (Chapter 2)	1. 2. 3.	1. 2. 3.	
Audiovisual and Visual Aid Mistakes (Chapter 3)	1. 2. 3.	1. 2. 3.	
Motivation Mistakes (Chapter 4)	1. 2. 3.	1. 2. 3.	

Mistake Category (Chapter in *Crash and Learn*)	My Top Three Mistakes Are:	My Action Steps Include:	I'm Committed to Correcting These Mistakes Because:
Difficult Participant Mistakes (Chapter 5)	1. 2. 3.	1. 2. 3.	
Co-Facilitation Mistakes (Chapter 6)	1. 2. 3.	1. 2. 3.	
Storytelling Mistakes (Chapter 7)	1. 2. 3.	1. 2. 3.	
Evaluation Mistakes (Chapter 8)	1. 2. 3.	1. 2. 3.	
Presentation Mistakes (Chapter 9)	1. 2. 3.	1. 2. 3.	

Additional Resources

Published Resources

Antion, T. (1999). *Wake 'Em Up! How to Use Humor and Other Professional Techniques to Create Alarmingly Good Business Presentations.* Landover Hills, MD: Anchor Publishing.

Arch, D. (1995). *Showmanship for Presenters.* Minneapolis: Creative Training Techniques Press.

Bowman, S. (2005). *Preventing Death by Lecture!* Glenbrook, NV: Bowperson Publishing Company.

Brockett, R.G., and R. Hiemstra. (1991). *Self-Direction in Adult Learning.* London: Routledge.

Brody, M. (2005). *Speaking Is an Audience-Centered Sport.* 3d edition. Jenkintown, PA: Career Skills Press.

———. (2006). *Effective Presentation Skills: Revitalize Your Speaking Style.* CD-ROM. Jenkintown, PA: Career Skills Press.

Buzan, T. (1991). *Use Both Sides of Your Brain.* New York: Penguin Group.

Candy, P.C. (1991). *Self-Direction for Lifelong Learning. A Comprehensive Guide to Theory and Practice.* San Francisco: Jossey-Bass.

Dryden, G., and J. Vos. (1999). *The Learning Revolution.* Fawnskin, CA: Jalmar Press.

Hall, D. (1996). *Jump Start Your Brain.* Clayton, South Victoria, Australia: Warner Books.

Hoff, R. (1992). *I Can See You Naked.* Kansas City, MO: Andrews & McMeel.

Jensen, E., and M. Dabney. (2001). *The New Science of Teaching.* San Diego: Brain Store.

Kirkpatrick, D.L., and J.D. Kirkpatrick. (2005). *Evaluating Training Programs: The Four Levels,* 3rd edition. San Francisco: Berrett-Koehler Publishers.

Knowles, M.S., E.F. Holton, R.A. Swanson, and E. Holton. (1998). *The Adult Learner.* Houston: Gulf Publishing.

Mager, R. (1992). *What Every Manager Should Know About Training.* Belmont, CA: Center for Effective Performance.

Mager, R., and P. Pipe. (1999). *Analyzing Performance Problems: Or You Really Oughta Wanna.* Belmont, CA: The Center of Effectiveness Performance.

Margolis, F.W., and C. Bell. (1989). *Understanding Training: Perspectives and Practices.* San Francisco: Pfeiffer & Company.

Merriam, S.B., and R.S. Caffarella. (1998). *Learning in Adulthood: A Comprehensive Guide,* 2nd edition. San Francisco: Jossey-Bass.

Putzier, J. (2001). *Get Weird: 101 Ways to Make Your Company a Great Place to Work.* New York: AMACOM.

Scannell, E., and J.W. Newstrom. (1998). *The Big Book of Business Games and The Big Book of Presentation Games.* New York: McGraw-Hill.

Seligman, M. (1998). *Learned Optimism: How to Change Your Mind and Your Life.* Roseburg, OR: Pocket Books.

von Oech, R. (1998). *A Whack on the Side of the Head.* Clayton, South Victoria, Australia: Warner Books.

Walters, L. (1993). *Secrets of Successful Speakers.* New York: McGraw-Hill.

Online Resources

Allison Manswell: www.allisonmanswell.com

ASTD: www.astd.org

CRM Learning: www.crmlearning.com

International Society for Performance Improvement: www.ispi.org

JIMPACT Enterprises: www.jimpact.com

The Learning Agenda: www.learningagenda.com

LearningWare: www.learningware.com

National Speakers Association: www.nsaspeaker.org

Raimond Honig: www.raimondhonig.com

About the Author

Jim Smith Jr., according to the many thousands who have participated in his moving motivational keynote presentations and workshops, is one of the most energetic and passionate speakers to come along in recent time. He works hard to connect with his audiences, encouraging them and challenging them to be outstanding. His speaking style evolved from his ups and downs in corporate America, education, professional and college sports, parenting, and marriage. This journey has brought him from humble beginnings to being an inspiration to both national and international audiences.

Jim is president and chief executive officer of JIMPACT Enterprises. He works with his customers and clients in the areas of professional trainer development, leadership, motivation, inclusion, and professional development. Prior to forming JIMPACT, he worked in leadership positions for the Bob Pike Group, Simmons Associates, CoreStates Bank, the Vanguard Group of Investments, and Prudential's American Association of Retired Persons (AARP) Operations. His current clients include MetLife, Commerce Bank, Subaru, Johnson & Johnson, AstraZeneca, and PEMCO. He is known for building performance, building relationships, and tapping into his learners' personal power.

A sought-after motivational speaker, Jim is the author of the best-selling book *From Average to Awesome: 41 Plus Gifts in 41 Plus Years* (2005, Beaver's Pond Press) and a co-author (along with Ken Blanchard, Mike Van Hoozer, Jack Canfield, John Christensen, and others) of the leadership book *The Masters of Success* (2006, Insight Publishing). He has received the Vanguard Group's Award of Excellence, the Philadelphia

INROADS Frank C. Carr Award (for community service), and recently was inducted into Temple University's Gallery of Success.

Jim has been called "Mr. Energy" and "The Trainer's Trainer." Just watch him in action, and you'll see why.

If you know of other mistakes committed by trainers and presenters that make you want to sleep, shout, or sneak out, please let Jim know. You may contact him via email at jimsmithjr@jimpact.com or visit his website (www.jimpact.com).

Index

THE *ASTD* MISSION:

Through exceptional learning and performance, we create a world that works better.

The American Society for Training & Development provides world-class professional development opportunities, content, networking, and resources for workplace learning and performance professionals.

Dedicated to helping members increase their relevance, enhance their skills, and align learning to business results, ASTD sets the standard for best practices within the profession.

The society is recognized for shaping global discussions on workforce development and providing the tools to demonstrate the impact of learning on the organizational bottom line. ASTD represents the profession's interests to corporate executives, policy makers, academic leaders, small business owners, and consultants through world-class content, convening opportunities, professional development, and awards and recognition.

Resources
- *T+D (Training + Development)* Magazine
- ASTD Press
- Industry Newsletters
- Research and Benchmarking
- Representation to Policy Makers

Networking
- Local Chapters
- Online Communities
- ASTD Connect
- Benchmarking Forum
- Learning Executives Network

Professional Development
- Certificate Programs
- Conferences and Workshops
- Online Learning
- CPLP™ Certification Through the ASTD Certification Institute
- Career Center and Job Bank

Awards and Best Practices
- ASTD BEST Awards
- Excellence in Practice Awards
- E-Learning Courseware Certification (ECC) Through the ASTD Certification Institute

Learn more about ASTD at www.astd.org.
1.800.628.2783 (U.S.) or 1.703.683.8100
customercare@astd.org

080615.31410